Creativity as a Bridge Between Education and Industry

Fostering New Innovations

David Tanner Ph.D.

Fredricka Reisman Ph.D.

**Includes E. Paul Torrance's creativity
teachings and insights in education**

Creativity As A Bridge Between Education
and Industry Fostering New Innovations
Copyright 2014 by David Tanner and Fredricka Reisman.
All rights reserved.

ISBN: 1497482992
ISBN 13: 9781497482999

Dedication

To the memory of Dr. E. Paul Torrance, pioneer and
champion of creativity in education.
and
To people in all functions of an organization who are
motivated to learn and apply creative thinking techniques that foster new innovations.

Acknowledgements

We are grateful to the following:
Creativity scholars upon whose work this book found much of its essence;
namely, Paul Torrance, Robert Sternberg, James Kaufman, and Keith
Sawyer.

Edward de Bono, Ned and Ann Herrmann, and Michael Kirton, whose
lectures and workshops stimulated DuPont company employees to learn
and apply the many creative thinking techniques described in this book.
We appreciate their permission to include this material in the book.

The American Creativity Association that motivated the authors to stay
active in the field of creativity and innovation over the years.

Tom Thaves for kindly giving permission to use the Frank and Ernest
cartoons in this book.

CreateSpace for help in designing the contents of this book.

Contents

I.

INTRODUCTION

Creative new innovations are urgently needed in education and industry. Knowledge gained in industry related to the field of creativity and innovation has potential value when applied in education, and likewise, knowledge gained in education has potential value when applied in industry. This book describes the value of creativity as a bridge between education and industry in fostering new bottom-line innovations.

In education, many colleges and universities preparing teachers and school administrators for future endeavors pay little attention to the field of creativity and innovation. They are experiencing criticism from many arenas, including from Arthur Levine who is a highly respected educator and former Dean of Teachers' College at Columbia University and who now heads up the Woodrow Wilson Foundation. Levine took a lot of heat for his on-target assessment of the state of teacher preparation; namely, that it is archaic and stuck in the ivory tower. Not only do teachers squelch kids' creativity, but tragically, they do not recognize their students' nor their own creative strengths. E. Paul Torrance, a renowned educator and international leader in creativity research, also found that teachers often inhibit rather than enhance and nurture students' creativity (Ref. 35). .

In industry, many companies are actively seeking new innovations in order to have a strong competitive position required for long-term survival and growth. Numerous articles are published in magazines, newspapers and journals about important innovations. But these publications communicate relatively little about the vital role of creative thinking in successful innovations. A world-wide study by IBM that surveyed 150 CEOs found that creativity is the most important competence for future leaders. If companies are to build a creative workforce, then K -12 schools and institutions of higher education need to start producing more creative thinkers.

Innovation in education and industry encompass many components related to creativity management that are vital to the innovation process. This book communicates knowledge about important components that bridge both education and industry:

- Sources of innovation;

- The role and characteristics of creative innovation champions;

- Creative thinking tools, processes, and frameworks that provide the fuel to ignite new innovations;

- A creative problem-solving process that plays an important role in the innovation process.

- The value of diverse thinking preferences and styles in building creative problem-solving teams.

- A process for fostering a culture for creativity and innovation in an organization;

- Structures and systems that sustain momentum in total creativity management;

- Teachings of E. Paul Torrance, renowned leader of creativity in education;

- Innovative stories ranging from "Kevlar" to crawfish bait that illustrate key components of the innovation process.

- A diagnostic creative intervention-mediation process that integrates three foci: diagnostic teaching; creativity; and mediation skills.

There are many definitions of creativity and innovation. For the purpose of this book, we define creativity as "the generation of novel, useful ideas." We define innovation as "taking best ideas to market." Innovation is the bottom line, but it won't occur without the generation of novel, useful ideas. Thus, creativity is generating original ideas; innovation is implementing these ideas.

The goal of this book is to cross-fertilize knowledge about creativity and innovation gained in education with that gained in industry. This book describes the brilliant teachings of Dr. E. Paul Torrance, renowned leader of creativity in education as well as other giants in the discipline of creativity.

A variety of non-biblical proverbs are cited throughout the book that communicate timeless wisdoms and express traditionally held truths about topics discussed. Proverbial wisdoms quoted in the text are listed in Appendix 3. Ref. 79 describes timeless proverbs and their origins.

This book contains many Frank and Ernest cartoons by Bob Thaves that appeared in - "Are We Creative Yet?" - , a book published in 1990 by E.I. DuPont de Nemours & Company and reprinted in 2005 by the American Creativity Association's ACA Press (Ref. 4, 5).

This book contains some material extracted from three prior David Tanner books on creativity and innovation (Ref. 1, 2, 3), and several Fredricka Reisman publications (Ref. 37, 43-46).

We hope that this book will be of value to innovators in both industry and education striving to bring new innovations to reality.

II.

SOURCES OF INNOVATION

All innovations are either Discovery-Driven or Needs-Driven.

Discovery-Driven Innovation

Discovery-driven innovation occurs when a fortuitous accident or unexpected event is observed leading to an invention that an observant creative thinker might formulate into a new innovation. There are many examples of this type of innovation including: Alexander Fleming's invention of penicillin, Alfred Nobel's invention of dynamite, and Roy Plunkett's invention of "Teflon."

The following cartoon exemplifies discovery-driven innovation.

Serendipity

Reprinted with permission, Frank and Ernest Cartoons cc Thaves

Needs-Driven Innovation

Needs-driven innovation occurs when creative thinkers identify an important need and respond by generating ideas to meet that need, and then take the best idea to reality.

This cartoon exemplifies needs-driven innovation:

Needs-Driven Innovation

Reprinted with permission, Frank and Ernest Cartoons cc Thaves

Both sources of innovation are important and both are influenced by a culture that supports the environment for creative thinking and innovation. But needs-driven innovations are more prevalent. They are triggered by a need recognized by a creative thinker or an organization that takes steps to generate ideas to meet the need.

Everyone is familiar with this well-known proverb pertinent to needs-driven innovation:

Necessity is the mother of invention

The origin of this proverb goes back to the days of Plato. It is based on the line *"Necessity, who is the mother of invention"* in *The Republic*, written by Plato, the Greek author and philosopher, 427-347BC, and remains a vital insight today. This proverb means that when people really need to do something in a serious situation, they will figure out a way to do it. For example, when the fan belt in a young ladies car broke in the middle of a deserted area, she used her stocking as a replacement. Not all situations necessitate such emergency actions, but there are many serious situations in industry and education necessitating action-oriented creative solutions. Creative thinkers play a vital role in championing these needs-driven solutions.

All sources of innovation are vital to support a strong competitive position of a business or advances in the education sector as reflected in this insight:

> Short-range, needs-driven innovations grow flowers; long-range, discovery-driven innovations grow trees. To fulfill a vision of a bright future, we need a landscape of both.

Innovation generally occurs in different time frames such as day-to-day, year-to-year, and decade-to-decade. In all cases a culture that promotes creative thinking plays a key role.

- *Day-to-day* innovation generally involves people at all levels of the organization generating ideas to meet a need on a daily basis. For example, a marketing person might think of a creative idea of how to convince a customer to buy his or her product.

- *Year-to-year* innovation involves major shifts in existing conditions, such as an organization introducing incremental new products, processes, or organizational structures. For example, DuPont developed a stain resistant carpet fiber to meet the need to develop soil-resistant carpets.

- *Decade-to-decade* innovation involves a step-change new technology or organizational re-structuring. The "Kevlar" innovation described in Chapter XI fits this category.

In all time frames, innovations are ignited by a creative new idea, concept, or discovery. Initiatives in creative thinking by individuals, teams, and organizations help fuel an ongoing trail of needs-driven innovations.

The *"Honey Pot"* Story

A good example of needs-driven innovation in industry is the "Honey Pot" story, told by Dr. Edward Glassman, former head of the program for team effectiveness, Department of Biochemistry and Nutrition in the School of Medicine, in Chapel Hill, N.C.

The story begins with a description of a need to solve a problem. It stresses the value of bringing together a group of people with diverse backgrounds to generate ideas on how to solve the problem. It also illustrates that no idea, regardless of how it's generated, is too crazy or too wild.

The Story

Pacific Power and Light faced a significant problem every time there was an ice storm. Ice would collect on power lines and cause them to break from the weight. There was a need to solve this problem. The current response to this need was to send linemen out to climb the poles and shake the wires. This was an undesirable task, since it needed to occur at the least desirable time to climb the poles - when it was cold, damp, and icy.

In order to generate a better solution, PP&L got people with a variety of diverse backgrounds together to have a "brainstorming" session. During a break, the moderator heard a conversation between two linemen: *"I hate this job. I sure hope we come up with a better way to get the ice off the lines. Last week, in addition to almost falling off the pole, I was chased by a big brown bear for about two miles. He just wouldn't give up."*

Upon reconvening, the moderator retold the story he'd overheard. In response, one participant said - *"The answer is obvious. We need to train the bears to climb the poles and shake the wires."* Everybody laughed. Then another said, *"The bears wouldn't have to shake the wires, they are so heavy that their weight on the end of the pole would be sufficient to shake the ice off."* The group laughed again. *"It's impossible to train the bears to climb the pole"*, someone said. *"Well, then, we just have to make it natural for the bears to climb the pole. We'll put honey pots on top of the poles. The bears will climb the poles to get the honey, and knock the ice off at the same time,"* said another. *"But, then, they'll just get the honey in clear weather, and not climb the poles when it's icy"*, another answered. And to that someone said *"That's an easy problem to solve. You know all those helicopters the company just bought to shuttle executives around? Well, they'll just have to walk when it's icy. We'll fly the copters around, putting the honey pots on top of the poles after an ice storm, the bears will climb the poles, and the ice will be shaken off."*

Then a secretary who had been quiet for the whole morning chimed in. *"My husband used to be a chopper pilot in Vietnam, and he told me that the downdraft from these choppers is really something. If we just flew the choppers over the icy power lines, the downdraft should knock the ice off. No men; no bears; no honey pots - just the downdraft from the helicopters."*

As you might have guessed, her idea worked and that's how PP&L now removes ice from power lines.

Diagnostic Creative Intervention-Mediation Process (Ref. 36, 75)

A diagnostic Creative Intervention-Mediation Process used in education is pertinent to needs-driven innovation. It integrates three foci; namely, diagnostic teaching, creativity, and mediation skills. Diagnostic teaching is a creative problem solving instructional/learning model that is framed upon generic or core influences on learning (Ref. 80, 81, 82), in depth content knowledge, and pedagogy knowledge. Creativity theories and how their applications complement diagnostic teaching suggest ways in which individuals may integrate intervention strategies in identifying "real" needs-driven problems and pathways to their solutions. Intervention strategies presented in this book encompass concepts of mediation and creative conflict resolution.

Renowned Needs-Driven Creative Thinkers

Several prominent creative thinkers wrote books that became valuable classics in the area of needs-driven creative thinking.

E. Paul Torrance, recognized the need for creativity research. He was an international leader in this field and was best known for developing the *Torrance Tests of Creative Thinking* which are used in the business world and in education to assess individuals' capacity for creativity. Torrance wrote that, "by far the most exciting insight that has come from research into creative thinking abilities is that different kinds of children learn best when given opportunities to learn in ways best suited to motivation and abilities" (Ref. 50). He authored 88 books, more than 2,000 publications, created the *Torrance Tests of Creative Thinking* (Ref.47), the *Future Problem Solving Program International* (Ref. 51), and the *Incubation Curriculum Model*

(Ref. 53). Torrance's 2001 book, *Manifesto: A Guide to Developing a Creative Career*, includes the results of his 40-year study of creativity (Ref. 52). The teachings of E. Paul Torrance are described in Chapter IV.

Alex Osborn recognized the need for a group problem-solving technique which all members of the group could then participate in. This creative thinking led to the well-known process of *brainstorming* (Ref. 6). He also recognized the need for a process to solve problems in a systematic way and fathered the *creative problem-solving process* described in his book, *Applied Imagination* (Ref. 7).

Edward de Bono, in his book *Mechanism of Mind*, recognized the need to develop creative thinking tools to help people step outside their normal thinking patterns in dealing with difficult problems and searching for new opportunities (Ref. 8). Hence he developed *lateral thinking* and many other creative thinking tools (Ref. 9). He also recognized the need for a focused thinking process, which led to *The Six Thinking Hats* framework (Ref. 10). Lateral thinking and the Six Thinking Hats are discussed in Chapter VI.

Ned Herrmann recognized the need to integrate the scientific study of the brain with the study of creative human development. To meet this need, he invented the *Herrmann Brain Dominance Instrument* (HBDI). The basic concept of the Herrmann model, described in his two books (Ref. 11, 12), is that the brain is composed of four interactive quadrants, each representing a category of preferences. Taken together, these four quadrants form a "whole brain," which profiles a person's thinking and behavior. Whole Brain Thinking is discussed in Chapter VIII.

Michael Kirton recognized the need for an instrument that measures people's creativity styles. To meet this need, he developed the widely applied *Kirton Adaption-Innovation Inventory* (KAI). The KAI is described in numerous journal articles, theses and his book *Adaption- Innovation: In the Context of Diversity and Change* (Ref. 13). It is discussed in Chapter VIII.

III.

CREATIVITY THEORIES
RELEVANT TO INNOVATION
(REF. 43)

Integrating creativity within industry management and education must first begin with an awareness of key theoretical models most closely associated with the development and application of creativity in real world situations. These theories form the intellectual foundation of creativity—the body of knowledge that underlies instilling creative thinking and creativity application into innovation. This is not a chicken egg issue—the knowledge base comes first. This sequence of knowledge preceding application is most evident when corporations hire *creativity consultants*, often for large sums of money, and do not receive the guidance they expected.

For one to lead a corporation or a school district into a changing environment infused with creativity, more is needed than a dynamic personality and gift of gab. What is needed is an in depth knowledge of the decades of relevant creativity research that is based upon theories such as those presented below. Just as a teacher must know about learning and teaching theories as well as having skill in diagnosing and assessing their students' gaps in knowledge, those who are creativity leaders also must diagnose their clients' goals and, like teachers, either have or be able to create relevant creativity instructional tools and techniques to reach these goals.

This chapter summarizes the contributions of bedrock creativity theorists and the relevance of their main ideas to innovation. The chapter deals with two questions: 1. What are the creative processes used by creative people, and 2. What does a creative person look like.

What are the Creative Processes Used by Creative People?

Graham Wallas. Wallas' model contains five stages for creative thinking (Ref.59):

1. Preparation - focuses on the problem and explores the problem's dimensions

2. Incubation - subconscious mulling of the problem

3. Intimation – inkling that a solution is on its way

4. Illumination - discovery; "Eureka!"

5. Verification - focus on practicality, effectiveness, appropriateness.

Wallas's theory provides a structured approach to creative problem solving. Understanding this is essential especially when considering the development of a creativity and innovation structure or process in one's firm. The structure needs to provide time and involve a variety of employees.

Sid Parnes & Alex Osborn. Their approach is a 4-step creative problem solving model that focused on using creativity in advertising. Component stages include both divergent and convergent processes (Ref. 60):

1. Understanding the problem

2. Generating ideas

3. Planning for Action

4. Acceptance finding

This model provides another look at the creative problem solving process - (http://creatingminds.org/tools/brainstorming.htm). A solid understanding of the difference between divergent and convergent processes is important.

Mihaly Csikszentmihalyi. The focus here is on the interplay among the creative person (the individual), the domain (the discipline) and the field (the experts/gatekeepers). The individual is the innovation manager, the domain is the discipline of creativity, and the field is comprised of the gatekeepers, e.g., CEOs whose decisions either allow or inhibit individual and/or group innovation. This may help you influence change in your organization.

Csikszentmihalyi (Ref. 61) also introduced 'flow' experiences that are applied here in the context of innovation management. Flow involves energy that focuses attention and motivates action.

Teresa Amabile. Motivation is central to Amabile's research, finding that intrinsic motivation is more apt to generate creativity than extrinsic motivation (Ref. 62). Establish diverse teams, perhaps from different company departments, to foster different perspectives, exploration and debate. Teams should comprise variety in expertise, creative-thinking styles, and cognitive abilities. This leads to divergent ideas and innovative solutions.

What Does a Creative Person Look Like?

Ellis Paul Torrance. Building on Guilford's work, Torrance developed the Torrance Tests of Creative Thinking (Ref. 47) that is a psychometric approach to measuring creativity. It is still the most widely used creativity assessment world-wide. Managers of creativity and innovation are in a position to facilitate original thinking, fluency and flexibility of ideas, elaboration, smart risk taking, tolerance of ambiguity, and resistance to premature closure, when exposed to these concepts.

Robert J. Sternberg. Sternberg presented two ideas: His *Triarchic Theory of Human Intelligence* (Ref. 63, 64) proposes that creativity is a balance among three forms of thinking: analytical, creative, and practical. Innovation Managers often deal with training on *analytical* thinking that includes having to analyze, critique, judge, compare/contrast, evaluate, assess. *Creative* tasks deal with the ability to invent, discover, imagine, suppose, predict; and *practical* intelligence is involved in everyday problem solving.

Sternberg further compared creativity to investment activities of *buying low and selling high*. Investment theory highlights perseverance in selling one's creative idea(s). Innovation Managers need to do this both within their discipline and also in the context of the field (see Csikszentmihalyi previously).

Abraham Maslow (Ref. 65). Maslow's *Hierarchy of Human Needs*, pictured below, presents a ladder of needs beginning with the most basic physiological needs (e.g., food, water, shelter, clothing), the security needs, both physiological and safety, the need for love and belonging, the esteem level that deals with self-confidence (self-assurance) and self-efficacy (believing in your abilities), both of which are important for innovation managers to persevere and champion their ideas. Success results in confidence, and those lacking confidence may not be able to produce creative ideas. Thus, it is important for the manager to view making mistakes as an opportunity for learning and encourage sensible risk taking. Finally, there is the self-actualization level, which involves peak experiences realizing all inner potential.

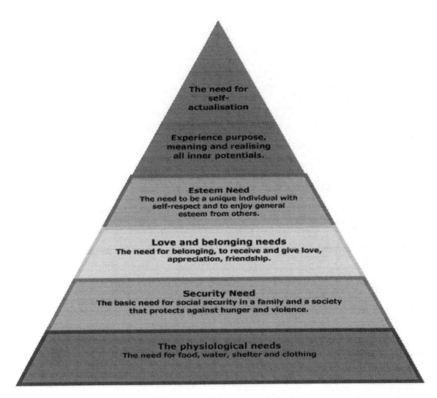

Maslow's Hierarchy of Needs

Carl Rogers (Ref. 66). Rogers avers that significant learning takes place when the task is perceived by the manager as having relevance for his or her own purposes. A role of an Innovation Manager is to facilitate innovation by: setting a positive climate for creative thinking, clarifying the purposes of team member roles, organizing and making available creativity resources, balancing intellectual and emotional components of creative endeavors, and sharing feelings and thoughts with colleagues but not dominating.

Howard Gardner (Ref. 67). Gardner developed a *theory of 'multiple intelligence' (MI)* which states that individuals have creative strength(s) that are domain-specific. When innovation managers become aware of Gardner's theory, they can reflect upon where they fall in the MI theory, and then coach others to become aware of their creative strengths. Gardner initially proposed eight intelligences: linguistic, logic-mathematical, musical, spatial, bodily/kinesthetic, interpersonal, intrapersonal, and naturalistic. He further stated a ninth, existential intelligence defined as the ability to use intuition to understand one's environment.

In summation, different perspectives of investigating creativity include a psychometric approach which focuses on assessing one's creative strengths (Torrance); a systems approach to understanding creativity (Csikszentmihalyi) which focuses on the individual, the domain (discipline), and the field (gatekeepers of an industry); the role of intrinsic and extrinsic motivation (Amabile) which states that intrinsic motivation yields more creative products; comparison with intelligence (Guilford, Sternberg); multiple intelligences (Gardner); humanistic psychology (Rogers, Maslow); and creative problem solving models (Wallas, Parnes). Mayer (Ref. 54) provides an excellent discussion of many assessment models and their proponents including psychometric methods, experimental methods, biographical methods, biological methods, computational methods and contextual methods.

IV.

E. PAUL TORRANCE TEACHINGS

E. Paul Torrance

Innovative Impact on Education

E. Paul Torrance was a renowned innovative educator and an international leader in creativity research. He is best known for developing the *Torrance Tests of Creative Thinking* (TTCT). These tests are used in the business world and in education to assess individuals' capacity for creativity. He defined creativity "as the process of sensing problems or gaps in information, forming ideas or hypotheses, testing and modifying these hypotheses, and communicating results" (Ref. 50).

In addition to developing the most widely used tests of creativity, Torrance also created the *Future Problem Solving Program* (Ref. 51), and developed the *Incubation Model of Teaching* (Ref. 53). He authored dozens of books and more than 2,000 published articles on creativity during the course of his career.

Torrace remained prolific after his retirement, writing several new books on creativity. Some of his best known books are *Guiding Creative Talent* (Ref. 68), The *Search for Satori and Creativity* (Ref. 70), The *Incubation Model of Teaching* (Ref. 57; 53), *Mentor Relationships and Why Fly?*(Ref. 69) His most recent books were such co-authored works as *Gifted and Talented Children in the Regular Classroom* (Ref. 71), *Multicultural Mentoring of the Gifted and Talented* (Ref. 72), *Making the Creative Leap Beyond* (Ref. 73), *Spiritual Intelligence: Developing Higher Consciousness* (Ref. 74), and the trilogy on *Learning Mathematics Creatively*(*Ref. 44, 45, 46*).

Torrance's 2001 book, *Manifesto: A Guide to Developing a Creative Career*, includes the results of his 40-year longitudinal study of creativity – the only one of its kind (Ref. 58).

The Torrance Manifesto

In the E. Paul Torrance *Manifesto for Children, Athens, GA: Georgia Studies of Creative Behavior and Full Circle Counseling, Inc.* Torrance stated the following:

- Don't be afraid to fall in love with something and pursue it with intensity.

- Know, understand, take pride in, practice, develop, exploit and enjoy your greatest strengths.

- Learn to free yourself from the expectations of others and walk away from the games they impose on you. Free yourself to play your own game.

- Find a teacher or mentor who will help you. Learn the skills of interdependence. Don't waste your time trying to be well rounded. Do what you love and can do well.

The Torrance Approach to Measuring Creativity

The highly reliable *Torrance® Tests of Creative Thinking* are described in the publisher's catalog (Scholastic Testing Service, Inc.) as the most widely used tests of their kind worldwide. These tests invite examinees to draw and give a title to their drawings (pictures) or to write questions, reasons, consequences and different uses for objects (words). These instruments have been used for identification of the creatively gifted and as a part of gifted matrices in states and districts in the USA, especially in multicultural settings, and for special populations around the world. Published in two equivalent forms, Forms A and B, the Figural and Verbal TTCT can be used for pre- and post-testing.

The **Figural TTCT**: Thinking Creatively with Pictures is appropriate at all levels, kindergarten through adult. It uses three picture-based exercises to assess five mental characteristics: fluency, elaboration, originality, resistance to premature closure, and abstractness of titles. The Figural TTCT can be scored locally or by STS and provides standardized scores for the mental characteristics listed above as well as for the following creative strengths: emotional expressiveness, internal visualization, storytelling articulateness, extending or breaking boundaries, movement or action, humor, expressiveness of titles, richness of imagery, colorfulness of imagery , synthesis of incomplete figures, synthesis of lines or circles, fantasy , and unusual visualization.

The Verbal TTCT®: *Thinking Creatively with Words* is appropriate for first graders through adults, and uses six word-based exercises to assess three mental characteristics: fluency, flexibility, and originality. These exercises provide opportunities to ask questions, to improve products, and to "just suppose."

A film, *Manifesto for Children*, documenting Torrance's life and work was broadcast on Georgia Public TV in the fall of 2000. The documentary focused on the longitudinal study which followed 215 young adults who attended two elementary schools in Minnesota from 1958 to 1964.

The students were given creativity tests each year and were followed up with a questionnaire in 1980. On the basis of their responses, the

Manifesto was developed to describe their ongoing struggle to maintain their creativity and use their strengths to create their careers and provide guidance to children.

In 1998, the participants were followed up to get a picture of their creative achievements and to validate the Manifesto. Some of the 101 respondents had attained eminence, while others had attained only mediocre careers.

"I suppose creativity is a part of intellect, but there are many abilities involved in intellect," said Torrance in a March 2001 Georgia Magazine story. "For the full development of creativity in children and adults, I am convinced they have a better chance in life if their best abilities are identified and encouraged.

"Originally, people thought a test could not be created. One issue was creating a test anyone could respond to – regardless of previous experiences. We did that and now the test has been translated into over 50 languages."

Heightened awareness of the importance of creativity led to the development of gifted programs all over the world. In Georgia, a student's success on the Torrance Tests is key to admission into gifted programs – which exist because every school system is charged with targeting students' learning levels.

Dr. Reisman, in collaboration with Dr. Torrance, administered the *Torrance Tests of Creative Thinking* (TTCT) to two classes of first graders in Athens, Georgia in 1970. These students had also taken the *Metropolitan Readiness Test*. Two little boys on the Metropolitan test scored in the intellectually disabled range, but on the TTCT, their scores were in the

120's—interpreted as highly creative. Their teachers, upon receiving the TTCT results said, "But these boys are such liars." Dr. Torrance replied that lying is a creative act and that they needed to be guided to use their creativity in more socially accepted ways. Thus, these young boys, originally slated for a special education track were now perceived positively by their teachers. The creativity results changed these children's lives.

The Torrance Incubation Model of Teaching

The following excerpt is from *Understanding Creativity: Where to Start?* (Ref.49).

The *Incubation Model of Teaching* (Ref. 57, 53) was developed as an instructional model. It is a three-stage model that provides opportunities for incorporating creative thinking abilities and skills into any discipline at any level from pre-school through professional and graduate education and the elderly.

This model consists of three stages: heightening expectations and motivation, deepening expectations or digging deeper, and going beyond or keeping it going.

The purpose of the first stage is to create the desire to know, to learn, or to discover; to arouse curiosity; to stimulate the imagination, and to give purpose and motivation.

The purpose of the second stage is to go beyond the surface and look more deeply into the new information. For creative thinking to occur, there must be ample opportunity for one thing to lead to another. This involves deferring judgment, making use of all the senses, opening new doors, and targeting problems to be considered or solutions to try.

The purpose of the third stage is to genuinely encourage creative thinking beyond the learning environment in order for the new information or skills to be incorporated into daily lives.

Those teachers who have applied this instructional model have reported that teaching becomes an exciting experience to them and to their students.

It can be applied not only to "teaching," but to lectures, sermons, workshops, seminars, and conferences.

This model was first applied on a large-scale in the Ginn Reading 360 (Ref. 55) and later to the 720 (Ref. 56). Field reports indicate that this program resulted in more reading, more books checked out of libraries, more seeking information through interviews and experiments, and discovery learning. Since the publication of the Incubation Model of Teaching (Torrance & Safter, 1990), it has been used in many other disciplines with reported success.

The Ideal Pupil

Torrance found that teachers often inhibit rather than enhance and nurture students' creativity (Ref.: 1975, Whitelaw, 2006). If companies are to build a creative workforce, then K -12 schools and institutions of higher education need to start producing creative and innovative thinkers.

Torrance developed a profile of the *ideal pupil* in regard to creative and productive constructs and developed a checklist for teachers and parents to assess what in their opinion was the ideal pupil/child. The checklist directions state:

> What kind of person would you like the children you teach to become? Please try to describe the kind of person you would like for your pupils to become by using the checklist of characteristics. Check each of the characteristics you think is generally desirable and should be encouraged. Then double check the characteristics you consider most important and should be encouraged above all others. Draw a line through those characteristics you consider undesirable and usually discourage.

> The checklist also allows teachers to substitute the following language depending upon population:

> a.   ...would you like your child to become?

> b.   ...would you like to become?

The Ideal Pupil/Child/Person Checklist is comprised of the following 66 characteristics:

1. Adventurous, testing limits	34. Never bored, always interested
2. Affectionate, loving	35. Submissive to authority
3. Altruistic, working for good of others	36. Persistent, persevering
4. Asking questions about puzzling things	37. Physically strong
5. Attempting difficult tasks	38. Popular, well-liked
6. Becoming Preoccupied with tasks	39 Preferring complex tasks.
7. Conforming	40. Quiet, not talkative
8. Considerate of others	41. Receptive of ideas to others
9. Courageous in convictions	42. Refined, free of courseness
10. Courteous, polite	43. Regressing occasionally, may be playful, childlike, etc.
11. Competitive, trying to win	44. Remembering well
12. Critical of others	45. Reserved
13. Curious, searching	46. Self-assertive
14. Desirous of excelling	47. Self-confident
15. Determined, unflinching	48. Self-starting, initiating
16. Disturbing procedures and and organization of the group	49. Ibid
17. Doing work on time	50. Sense of beauty
18. Domineering, controlling	51. Sense of humor
19, Feeling emotions strongly	52. Sincere, earnest
20. Emotionally sensitive	53. Socially well-adjusted
21. Energetic, vigorous	54. Spirited in disagreement

22. Fault-finding, objecting	55. Striving for distant goals
23. Fearful, apprehensive	56. Stubborn, obstinate
24. Guessing, hypothesizing	57. Talkative
25. Haughty and self-satisfied	60. Truthful, even when it hurts
26. Healthy	61. Unsophisticated, artless
27. Independent in judgment	62. Unwilling to accept things on mere say-so
28. Independent in thinking	63. Versatile, well-rounded
29. Industrious, busy	64. Visionary, idealistic
30. Intuitive	65. Willing to accept judgments of authorities
31. Liking to work alone	66.Willing to take risks
32. Neat and orderly	
33. Negativistic, resistant	

Interpretation of The Ideal Pupil/Child/Person Checklist

Torrance's interpretation of the checklist dealt with validation and reliability studies rather than direct interpretation. Thus, for purposes of interpretation, we have categorized the Ideal Pupil items in terms of 11 factors that comprise the Reisman Diagnostic Creativity Assessment (RDCA) discussed next. This approach allows for both additional diagnostic interpretation, as well as triangulation of the self-report RDCA with the generally accepted definitions of the Ideal Pupil terms.

These 11 factors or characteristics are discussed further in the section below.

The Reisman Diagnostic Creativity Assessment (RDCA)

Reisman has developed a new mobile phone application offered as an Apple App on iTunes that's built upon the Torrance Tests of Creative

Thinking. It's called the *Reisman **Diagnostic Creativity Assessi*** **(RDCA),** which assesses an individual's self-perception on 11 major ativity factors. The Torrance test can be scored by trained evaluators takes an hour or longer while the RDCA is automatically scored, takes about 10 minutes to complete and provides immediate results. It is still in development and undergoing factor analysis, validity and reliability testing.

The currently free RDCA may be accessed via iPad, iTouch or iPhone., It provides a (Likert-type) assessment resulting in a self-report designed to be used diagnostically to identify one's creative strengths, rather than to predict creativity. The RDCA results can be used to provide the assessment taker with the following infirmation: an instant creativity score; scores to identify specific creativity factors in which the taker may already be strong; factors they may be personally satisfied with and wish to strengthen through creativity exercises such as presented in this book. The 11 factors tapped by the RDCA are as follows:

1. Originality – unique and novel;

2. Fluency- generates many ideas;

3. Flexibility-generates many categories of ideas;

4. Elaboration-adds detail;

5. Tolerance of Ambiguity – comfortable with the unknown;

6. Resistance to premature closure – keeps an open mind;

7. Convergent Thinking- comes to closure;

8. Divergent thinking – generates many solutions (related to fluency);

9. Risk Taking – adventuresome;

10. Intrinsic Motivation – inner drive;

11. Extrinsic Motivation – needs reward or reinforcement.

Originality Thinking Strategies[1]

Examples for enhancing original thinking deal with practice in creating unique and novel outcomes. Activities for enhancing the other 10 creativity factors are under development. Strategies for enhancing original thinking follow:

1. **Atmosphere.** All of our senses -- what we see, hear, feel, taste, and touch -- influence our state of mind. A positive atmosphere contributes to a positive and creative state of mind. Some people thrive in loud, people-filled areas with much activity. Others need quiet and calm to think clearly and creatively. Find that place, noisy or quiet, that makes you feel comfortable, have them focus on their sensory input preferences, and engage in creative problem solving in the best atmosphere for them.

2. **Find a Place to Walk.** If you think best "on your feet," find a hallway, sidewalk, or park where you can walk. Wear comfortable shoes and clothing.

3. **Find a Place to Relax.** Set up your office or other room with a good chair, paintings, lighting, music, fresh flowers, and anything else that will help you relax.

4. **Use Pictures, Words, Sounds, Software for Inspiration.** Surround yourself with inspirational props. In coming up with a business name or an illustration idea or a hook for your next press release, you might use magazines, phone books, junk mail, cereal boxes, poetry, or crossword puzzles to generate ideas. Collect whatever materials inspire you -- that give you ideas. Even computer programs such as IdeaFisher can help you develop your natural creativity and foster creative thinking.

   Besides what we see or hear, the scents, textures, and tastes experienced during our creative thinking time contribute to our

---

[1]   Enhancement strategies for the other 10 factors as well as the originality factor are found in the RDCA Enhancement Strategies Manual under completion as an Apple App, authored by F.Reisman, L.Keiser and O. Otti, and published by Drexel University's Drexel-Torrance Center for Creativity and Innovation.

creativity. Both good and bad smells can trigger the ideas we need. Trying to come up with a name for a new food product? Smell it, taste it, hold it in your hands. Get all your senses involved in the process.

With a clear head and a clear space you can let your mind wander -- but not too much. To solve a problem you also need to direct creative thinking with some effective thinking.

5. **Effective Thinking.** While positive thinking allows your mind to accept new ideas and creative thoughts, effective thinking involves directing your thoughts toward specific goals. Daydreaming, relaxation, and free association allow the mind to come up with new or unusual ideas or idea fragments.

6. **Identify Your Creative Challenge.** Applied to creative thinking, originality involves clearly defining what creative challenge you need to meet. Do you want a new corporate logo? Are you looking for an unmet need to turn into a business? Are you trying to come up with an exciting or unusual direct mail piece within a limited budget? Whatever the challenge, direct your thoughts and activities toward that goal. Focus and awareness are key.

7. **Have a Goal for Your Creative Thinking.** Without a specific goal in mind, random thoughts and ideas may not be particularly useful. Gerald Kushel, Ed.D., author of Effective Thinking for Uncommon Success, in a 1991 interview for Bottom Line Personal newsletter, said that to be an effective thinker, you need to have goals and a commitment to those goals. He outlines four steps toward effective thinking:

i. Take Notice. Take stock of where you are or what you are doing. Is it moving you toward your goal?

ii. Pause. Take a break when you get off-track.

iii. Identify Effective Thoughts. When a thought enters your head, identify it as effective or defective, positive or negative.

iv. Choose. We can choose our thoughts. It's the underlying premise of positive thinking. It's true of effective thinking and creative thinking, as well. Choose to focus on those thoughts that bring you closer to your goals.

8. **Creativity takes practice.** Your creativity is there within you, but you must make a habit of using your imagination. Although many of your best ideas will come when you "aren't really concentrating," you can make them happen more often by regularly practicing effective thinking techniques.

9. **Schedule Creative Thinking.** Even when not pondering a specific creative challenge, set aside a certain amount of time each day, week, or month to relax, brainstorm, and daydream. Make creative thinking a habit. By getting in the habit of scheduling regularly creativity thinking time and creativity exercises you'll be better able to meet future challenges as they arise.

10. **Ponder On Problems That Don't Exist.** This isn't the same as worrying about things you can't change or trying to fix what isn't broken. It means that even when you've come up with the perfect path to achieve your goals, think about alternatives. Keep a file of ideas that were discarded as not feasible this time around. You may find inspiration for solving future problems and creative challenges. Keep the sketches that the client rejected or that you never even showed to them. Sometimes pulling out these old ideas will generate new ones when needed. And keeping a file of ideas that were rejected doesn't mean just holding them in your head.

11. **Write it down. Make Notes Any Time, Any Place.** Get in the habit of making notes, outlines, sketches, or doodles. If you are actively pursuing a specific idea or problem, always have paper and pencil or recorder at the ready. Jot down or record all your thoughts, no matter how "off-the-wall."

12. **Keep a Notebook By Your Bed.** Some of your best thoughts come just before falling asleep and just after waking. Keep a notebook at your bedside so you will always be ready to write down ideas whenever they come.

13. **Create an Inspiration File.** Whether it's a file folder, a note-book, or an entire file cabinet, keep clippings, thumbnail sketches, junk mail, photos, and anything else that inspires you or gives you ideas. Add the notes you regularly take. Don't just file it and for-get it - go through the file culling your scheduled creative think-ing times and when actively pursuing ideas for a project.

14. Brutethink

The idea of the Brutethink creative thinking technique is that by forc-ing a random idea into a challenge or problem situation, you produce out of the ordinary choices to solve your problem (Ref.77: Michalko, 2006:157–169). Steps in the Brutethink process are as follows:

1. Bring a random word into the problem (from a dictionary, newspaper, book...);

2. Think of things associated with the random word;

3. Force connections between the random word and the challenge, also between the associated things and the challenge;

4. List all your ideas.

Thus, this strategy uses a list of words to provoke original think-ing, utilizing unlikely comparisons to stimulate idea production. Michalko provides several pages of that work well for this purpose (Ref. 77, pages 159-172). Michalko gives the example of someone try-ing to improve a relationship with a boss. They select the word "pen-cil" and begin a list of connections they might never have thought of otherwise. Michalko stresses the importance of selecting words that are truly random so as to "spark a free association of ideas."

Challenge: In what ways may I improve my relations with my manager? Random word: *pencil*

The following table shows the sequence of connections toward solving the challenge:

Application of Brutethink

Words to Connect	Connecting Ideas to Challenge Problem
Eraser	Erase past failures
Shaft	I'm getting the shaft. He gives me too much work. I need help.
Yellow	I am uncomfortable to talk with him about my career at work. Maybe we'll get some coffee after work.
Lead	Get the lead out. His support is always too little and too late.
Gold circle	He doesn't think I/m going after the important clients. How can I disprove this?
Cheap	Our commission plan is lower than the industry level. Perhaps I should suggest a new plan.
Six sides to a pencil	The six most important things to address are: improve communication, seriously discuss my career, propose new commission plan, prioritize accounts, improve time management, and create new ways for account follow-up.

15. Random Words

This activity is similar to Brutethink presented previously. It is used to stimulate fluency of creative new ideas and divergent thinking. The following steps are involved:

(1) *Find a random word* that will be used as a stimulus for new ideas by looking around your environment and see what words are triggered. Open a book to a random page and select a stimulus word. Good random words are (a) evocative and (b) have little relation to the challenge under consideration. Nouns, verbs, and adjectives can all be used effectively.

(2) *Find associations* that involve relating the random word to other concepts. Continue generating associations until a creative topic emerges.

(3) *Use the associations to create new ideas* by linking any of the associations with your challenge.

Steps 2 and 3 may work together by finding an association and an immediate idea from it, thus pushing you to think in new ways and create novel ideas.

V.

CREATIVE INNOVATION
CHAMPIONS

A creative innovation champion in the context of this book, is a creative thinker who identifies an important need, participates in generating novel, useful ideas to meet the need, and plays a key role in taking the best idea to market. Innovations succeed because of the drive, determination and tenacity of creative innovation champions.

An important component of innovation management in industry and education is to provide space and freedom for needs-driven creative innovation champions. This chapter describes their role and general characteristics.

Role

The first step in needs-driven innovation occurs when a creative innovation champion identifies a high priority need. The next step is idea generation to meet that need. It's essential for the champion to have a clear understanding of the need before undertaking steps to meet the need. Sometimes he or she must dig deeper than what's on the surface, as illustrated in this parable (author unknown):

> Long ago in a distant land lived a baker of some distinction. He was considered by many to be the finest designer and decorator of cakes and pastries in the entire kingdom of Businessland. As it happened, the king

33

of Businessland decided to hold a party for his fiftieth birthday and sent word to the baker to prepare for the celebration the largest and most wonderful birthday cake ever seen in the kingdom. The baker was delighted that the king had chosen him for such a high honor and immediately set out with great anticipation to design a magnificent masterpiece. He immediately ordered twelve dozen eggs from the old women who owned the chicken farm up the road, along with three sacks of sugar and twenty pounds of chocolate from the confectioner. When these arrived, he began mixing his cake. He measured out the sugar, added the eggs, and began to add the flour only to find that he did not have enough to make such a large cake. He ran down the street to the miller only to find that the miller had closed his shop and left town for the week to visit his mother in Wilmingham.

Fortunately for the baker, he was able to purchase more flour from the bread maker, who charged him dearly since he knew how important this order was to the baker and that the miller was out of town. He prepared the rest of his batter and poured his handiwork into the molds that he had carefully handcrafted. He moved the molds over to his oven and to his great horror found that the molds for such a large and wonderful cake would not fit into the oven. He was greatly distressed, but did not despair for long. He found a large hammer and began smashing away at the oven. Within a few hours he had broken away the top of the oven and began the task of rebuilding the oven with a higher ceiling. Finally the oven was finished and he moved his precious molds into the oven. Soon the cake was finished and he moved the molds to his decorating area where he worked furiously to craft a cake of unparalleled beauty and awe.

He rushed the cake over to the royal castle only to find that the celebration had already begun. Undaunted, he paraded the magnificent cake into the ballroom to the gasps and wonderment of the excited guests. To his absolute horror the king frowned, groaned, and announced angrily, "I hate chocolate!" The baker was thrown out of the castle and never heard from again.

This parable illustrates how an important needs-driven innovation can be fraught with unexpected outcomes, surprises, and setbacks. It punctuates the importance of the creative innovation champion to understand and define the "core" need before undertaking a project. A diagnostic assessment of the king's likes and dislikes could have led to a more positive situation.

Characteristics of Creative Innovation Champions

While people's thinking styles and behavior patterns differ, there are certain characteristics that most creative innovation champions have in common. They generally embody some, if not all, of the eight important characteristics listed below and described in this section.

1. Discontent with the Status Quo.

2. Open Minded

3. A "Prepared" Mind

4. Positive Thinking

5. Willing to Take Risks

6. Action-Oriented

7. Persistent

8. Hard Working

1. Discontent with the Status Quo

Creative innovation champions have an absolute discontent with the status quo. Hence, they constantly search for ways to constructively improve current practices. These people are sometimes viewed as "trouble-makers, " but they often come up with the most creative ideas and drive them to reality. People don't have to be troublemakers to be creative thinkers.

Sometimes, great things materialize from small needs-driven actions of an innovation champion discontent with the status quo as expressed in this proverb:

Mighty oaks from little acorns grow.

This proverb was expressed in an essay by D. Everett in the Columbia Orator, 1797: *"Large streams from little fountains flow, tall oaks from little acorns grow."*

Little acorns don't always grow into mighty oaks, but creativity-driven acorns in industry and education often lead to a sequence of events that impact the personal lives, far and wide, of a great many people.

2. Open Minded

Creative innovation champions seek alternative innovative solutions to meet an important need. They don't grab at the first idea, but take time to search for alternatives. The creative thinking techniques discussed in Chapter IV., such as lateral thinking and metaphoric thinking, are helpful to creative thinkers searching for alternative solutions to difficult problems.

3. A Prepared Mind

Creative innovation champions have a "prepared" mind and are alert to things around them that might trigger ideas to meet important needs. Many discoveries often attributed to circumstances or luck occur because the creative thinker had a "prepared" mind. The invention of spunbonded sheet structures, and discovery of a dye resistant nylon carpet fiber described in Chapter IV were the result of creative researchers having a prepared mind.

Famous examples are Alexander Fleming's invention of penicillin, Alfred Nobel's invention of dynamite, and Roy Plunkett's invention of "Teflon." A prepared mind also is evident in the comedic process of translating daily observations to comedy club shtick.

4. Positive Thinking

Creative innovation champions are positive thinkers. They look forward, not backward. It's a state of mind that plays a vital role in driving forward new bottom-line innovations. Positive thinking often involves viewing a negative from different angles and turning it into a positive, illustrated by the following story.

> *Two shoe companies each sent a representative to a developing country to help decide whether to build a shoe factory. The first representative wired back - Nobody wears shoes here, don't build factory. The second representative was a creative thinker and wired back - NOBODY WEARS SHOES HERE... OPPORTUNITY UNLIMITED... BUILD LARGE FACTORY!!*

The following cartoon, which views a curved flashlight beam as a problem with worn batteries could be viewed instead as the discovery of a flashlight that shines around corners.

Printed with permission, Frank and Ernest Cartoons ccThaves

Positive Psychology, related to "positive thinking", is discussed later in this chapter.

5. Willing to Take Risks

Creative innovation champions are willing to take risks. Risk-taking requires courage. People are often fearful of risk-taking, which is perfectly normal. John McCain, in his book, *Why Courage Matters*, comments:

Courage is not the absence of fear, but the capacity for action despite our fear

Risk-taking is the spirit fostering innovation. Creative thinkers are willing to take risks when the needs-driven stake is high because they realize:

Nothing ventured, nothing gained.

The above proverb dates back to 14th century Chaucer and the French proverb - "He who never undertook anything never achieved anything." It refers to the wisdom that you can't get anywhere unless you are willing to take a risk.

Most successful creative thinkers realize that risk-taking doesn't need to be taking a "blind" chance. It can be taken as a well thought-out course of action. A management challenge is to create an environment of trust where failure is not punished, but learned from to aid future risk-taking successes.

6. Action-Oriented

Creative innovation champions motivated to accomplish a task realize that -

Actions speak louder than words.

What you do is more important than what you say. Often it's important for innovation champions to take rapid action because -

A stitch in time saves nine

This proverb refers to a garment where one stitch in time could save the need for nine stitches later on. Innovation champions realize the value of not procrastinating because timely innovations can fix a problem before it becomes larger and harder to fix.

Alan Bean, former U.S. astronaut and respected adventurer made the following statement in a talk he gave at a Creativity Week meeting held at the Center for Creative Leadership in Greensboro, NC:

> *When you have a good idea, don't spend a lot of time talking about it or asking permission, just go out and do it!*

7. Persistent

Successful creative innovation champions are persistent in pursuing their needs-driven innovations. Obstacles frequently arise, but the following proverb captures their attitude:

> **If at first you don't succeed, try, try again**

This proverb is traced back to several sources in the 18th century. It makes the point that persistence pays off. Don't let a first time failure stop further attempts.

The comedian W. C. Fields is quoted as saying:*" If at first you don't succeed, try, try again. Then quit. There's no point in being a damn fool about it."*

Innovation champions realize that if the chance of success has a high stake, only a fool would quit!! They know when they have an important innovation to pursue and *"champion"* for it. If questioned, they don't give up, but are persistent in aggressively seeking ways to sell and pursue their innovation.

Printed by permission, Frank and Ernest cartoons ccThaves

A good example is described in Chapter XI where the idea of crawfish bait was initially rejected by the business unit as not being pertinent to their current business. The champions created suction for the product by giving samples to fisherman, which then created a demand for the product.

Persistent creative thinkers also realize that:

A journey of a thousand miles begins with the first step.

This proverb is attributed to Confucius. It means that a long journey can seem overwhelming until you start it. Take enough single steps and perhaps you'll arrive.

Some innovations take a long time to bring to reality because of resistance to change. In 1513 Machiavelli wrote:

There is nothing more difficult than to take the lead in the introduction of a new order of things. The innovator has for enemies all who have done well under the old conditions, and lukewarm defenders in those who may do well under the new.

8. Hard Working

Observations over years in industry and education have led to the conclusion that, of the many characteristics listed, only one was common to all creative innovation champions:

An intense interest in working hard at what they were doing.

This characteristic is prevalent in needs-driven creative thinkers who work long, hard hours to move their innovations toward reality.

This characteristic is exemplified by the manufacturing person described in Chapter VI who lay in his bed with the plant problem "throbbing in his head like a toothache." He dreamed of a possible solution, and went to work before sunrise to try it.

The eight characteristics described in this section are not necessarily innate. To be a successful creative innovation champion it helps for a person to: question the status quo; seek alternative solutions to problems;

have a "prepared" mind; think positively; be action-oriented; recognize that nothing ventured, nothing gained; be persistent in championing and aggressively pursuing their objectives; and - most importantly - *work hard at it.*

Several innovations ranging from "Kevlar" to crawfish bait are described in Chapter XI which reflect the characteristics of successful innovation champions.

Positive Psychology

Dr. Martin Seligman of the University of Pennsylvania and a President of the American Psychological Association called for innovative researchers to focus efforts on understanding *positive psychology.* Positive psychology, related to "positive thinking", broadens the research focus of psychologists to include identifying and nurturing peoples' talents rather than only dealing with disease and disorder.

Positive Psychology is described by Professor Seligman as "the scientific study of the strengths and virtues that enable individuals and communities to thrive. " In regard to the workplace, Seligman found that human strengths (rather than the absence of human weaknesses) are the keys to productivity, to resistance to the negative effects of stress, to increased job satisfaction, lower turnover and absenteeism, and to increased customer satisfaction.

Positive psychology has some central components described in the following table:

Components of Positive Psychology

Optimism	Gratitude	Emotional Resilience	Flow	Creativity
Monitor our thoughts, what are we thinking about? Are these self-defeating thoughts or are they positive thoughts.	Be aware of situations, people, things that we are thankful for.	Define what it is that makes some people succeed against all odds and what is it that makes others succumb to failure?	*Flow* is a state in which a person becomes fully immersed in involvement, of an activity. The term was popularized by Mihaly Csikszentmihalyi.	There are several qualities that set leaders apart: The willingness to do the right thing (rather than what is expedient at the moment); challenging employees to work at a high level of professionalism; encouragement for employees to think for themselves and be creative; and development of employee skills and abilities to enable them to fully utilize their inborn talents.

Optimism Activities:

Write five or six positive things about yourself on a card and then read them every day (e.g., I am a good team player, I am a good manager, I am a good dad/mom/sister/brother, whatever things in your life, you feel are positive).

Laugh a little bit. When we laugh, we increase our Serotonin, Dopamine level of brains and actually we feel a little bit better.

Managers, in particular, should understand how individual employees respond to optimism. Some people need a relationship, some people want to be encouraged, some people need clear goals, strategies for increasing gratitude, some need to be left alone.

Gratitude Activity. Write down three things that you actually are happy about everyday and that you feel thankful for. Managers may compare their list with employees and begin to create unison in gratitude beliefs.

Emotional Resilience Activity. Practice perseverance, do not give-up, learn from experiences. Share experiences of perseverance

Flow Activities. Engage in positive thoughts that can turn into positive actions. Athletes experience flow when they are in the midst of excelling at their sport, musicians can lose themselves in their composition, scholars can get lost in thought.

Creativity Activity. Do things a little bit differently, even though it might be threatening. Positive psychology is about risk, it doesn't mean we are going to succeed every time. It means that, if we don't take a risk, we will guarantee that we won't succeed.

VI.

CREATIVE THINKING AS A SKILL

If you think creative thinking is a mysterious gift, you can only sit and wait for ideas. But, if creativity is a skill you ought to learn it."

- Edward de Bono

Donald W. MacKinnon, University of California writes:

> *During most of man's literate history, creative behavior has been thought to be artistic behavior and rather especially the writing of poetry, although the work of painter and sculptor were recognized early as being in the same class. The view that writing of poetry is a matter of artistry, has been expanded to include the idea that scientists as well as many others in their endeavors can also be creative persons employing as does the artist the creative process.*

The above quotation makes the salient point that not only poets, painters, and sculptors can be creative, but that all persons can think creatively as they pursue their endeavors. Creative thinking is an essential ingredient in all innovations and human endeavors, both in generating the original idea and in overcoming barriers to bring the idea to reality. Creative thinking does not replace information, training, logic or hard work, but is another factor in getting the job done better.

There is a myth that creativity is limited to a few individuals who are naturally creative. In reality, creativity is a skill. It's a skill that can be learned and applied like any other skill.

Research with fraternal and identical twins supports the view that different abilities to think creatively are not inherited (Ref. 13). Thinking and creative thinking are learnable skills like driving a car, swimming, golfing, or knitting. Some people will be better at certain things than others; but given sufficient motivation, instruction and practice, everyone can raise his or her level of skill.

Innovators seeking to generate ideas to meet a need will benefit by becoming acquainted with the many creative thinking techniques that are available. An important component of total innovation management is to facilitate the education process. Eighteen of the most productive creative thinking techniques and many examples of practical applications are described in this chapter. It is not intended as a comprehensive review, but rather a brief discussion of those techniques found to be productive in the workplace.

Creative thinking techniques can be categorized in many ways. One approach is to organize them into the following categories, all having value:

- Pattern-Breaking Tools;

- Idea-Generating Processes; and

- Focused Thinking Frameworks.

Pattern-Breaking Tools

In solving difficult problems and searching for new opportunities, our natural tendency is to build from our long-standing experience base. Often it works, but sometimes it doesn't. This type of approach - linear thinking - is important and a logical starting point, particularly in traditional cost-cutting and quality improvement programs. There is another approach. When our traditional, linear thinking methods do not bring the results we want, we need to look at things in a new way.

Breaking away from traditional thinking is more easily said than done. This is illustrated humorously in the movie, *Dead Poets Society*. In this movie, Robin Williams, an instructor at a prep school, tells students to tear out introductory pages in their poetry book. Tearing pages from a book goes against the norm. It's humorous to watch the students' shocked faces as they struggle against stepping outside the paradigm that tearing pages from a book is "sinful."

In another scene, Robin Williams demonstrates his approach to looking at the world differently. He tells his students to jump on top of his desk and look around from that vantage point. He comments:

Break out... look around you...dare to strike out and find new ground.

We don't have to jump on top of desks or tables to look at the world differently. There exist deliberate, systematic tools for creative thinking that help us break away from normal thinking patterns. These tools can be learned and applied as can any skill.

Six pattern-breaking creative thinking tools with examples of practical application are described below.

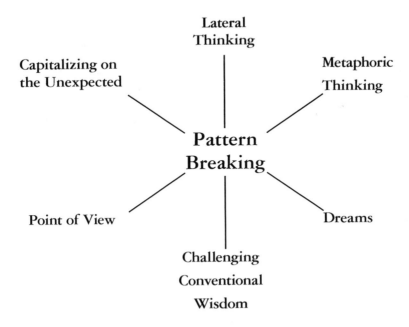

Lateral Thinking

Lateral thinking is perhaps the most productive tool to help break away from traditional thinking. It is described in several books by Dr. Edward de Bono (Ref. 9, 15-17) and taught in certification courses by de Bono Thinking Systems (Ref. 18). Lateral thinking is defined in the *Oxford English Dictionary:*

Seeking ways to solve problems by apparently illogical means.

Dr. Edward de Bono's book, *Mechanism of Mind,* first published in 1969 (Ref. 8), is a classic in the field of creative thinking. It explains that the mind is a self organizing information system. As our mind absorbs information and digests experiences, our thinking organizes itself into patterns based on these inputs.

Pattern thinking is essential. Otherwise, we would have to rethink each morning whether we put our shoes on before our socks or our socks on before our shoes. We would have to relearn how to walk. In tackling problems or searching for new opportunities, it is sensible to start out with normal patterns of thinking. This generally provides many useful ideas. But to solve difficult problems or conceive radically new concepts that require a new direction in thinking, it is often necessary to step outside our normal patterns of thinking. Some refer to this as "thinking outside the box."

Visualize, in the figure below, tackling a difficult problem and racing "linearly" down a highway going east, the direction of thinking that you perceive might lead to a solution.

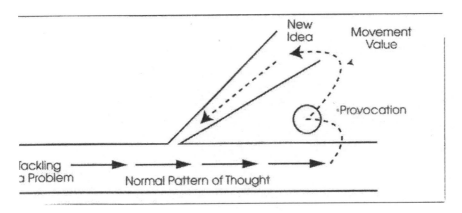

Reprinted with permission. c2012. I P Development Corporation.
Published by de Bono Thinking Systems

If there is a side road going north, you would likely speed past it, even though it might lead to a wider, faster highway and allows you to arrive at your destination more quickly.

There are ways to test these side roads in problem solving or opportunity searching that might lead to better, more novel ideas. A productive approach is to create "provocations" that jar us outside our normal patterns of thinking. Provocations are thoughts that are related to the issue being attacked, but that are illogical or unstable. They are bizarre, impractical, ridiculous, or provocative.

Instead of rejecting a provocation, we can learn to use it for its forward effect as a stepping-stone to shift laterally out of standard linear patterns of thinking. This process creates a new starting point to address the problem and always leads to a flow of new, useful ideas.

Dr. de Bono teaches several techniques that systematically help generate provocations:

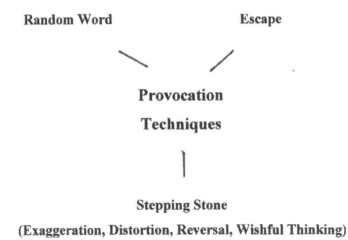

Random Word   **Escape**

Provocation

Techniques

Stepping Stone
(Exaggeration, Distortion, Reversal, Wishful Thinking)

Random Word involves creating a new "entry point" by selecting a word at random, e.g., a noun from a dictionary or poster that is not connected to the subject.

Escape involves examining the subject for what we take for granted and then canceling, negating, or escaping from some of the things we take for granted.

Stepping- stone involves the exaggeration, reversal, distortion, or wishful thinking about a subject that is a stepping-stone to new ideas.

Applications

The lateral thinking process involves three steps:

1. Selection of a focus area requiring creative new ideas.

2. Development of provocations relating to the focus area using lateral thinking techniques.

3. Generation of sensible ideas dealing with the problem stimulated by the provocation.

The bolder the provocation, the better the chance it will lead to many unusual ideas. The challenge is to generate several provocations and ideas until one rings a bell and excites enthusiasm. A productive lateral thinking session is one that generates at least one "great" idea worth implementing!

Learning the lateral thinking techniques is a first step. Applying this knowledge in a practical way after leaving the classroom or lecture is another matter. Several examples are described below to illustrate the lateral thinking process.

Innovative Cost Reduction

This example illustrates how a need to reduce costs led a team to apply lateral thinking to the issue and save over $500,000 annually.

A corporate information systems team was dealing with this need:

How can we reduce costs in the information systems function?

The group manager attended a lateral thinking workshop and decided to hold a meeting to apply her new knowledge to this problem. When the flow of ideas was exhausted using pattern thinking, she explained lateral thinking to the group. Many new ideas were generated.

The lateral thinking technique that paid off in this case was *reversal*. It led to this provocation:

Reduce costs by spending more money

This provocation generated the idea that spending more money on fewer equipment vendors would provide leverage to obtain large discounts. The approach was to cut the number of vendors and negotiate better prices on high-volume orders. This idea led to an annual savings of more than $300,000. The concept was applied to maintenance and saved a similar amount. Hence, a two-hour lateral thinking session provided an annual savings of over $500,000. Over a ten-year period, those savings would amount to over five million dollars.

Accelerated Plant Computerization

A plant technical group, working jointly with manufacturing and the engineering department, had developed a prototype for computerizing the complex "Nomex" plant process. They were at the stage of purchasing and installing plant-scale equipment. Ben Jones, an innovative technical manager, skilled in lateral thinking, convinced colleagues to have a creative problem-solving session to address this needs-driven challenge:

> *How can we install the computer system in the plant much faster and at a substantially lower cost than forecasted?*

The problem-solving session precipitated many provocations. The one that paid off used the "escape" technique:

> *Eliminate the Engineering Department*

This provocation led to the risky idea to skip the normal step of preassembling hardware and software at the Engineering Department Laboratory. Instead, they chose to ship the entire computer system directly to the plant where it would be integrated directly into the plant process. The team took the view - *nothing ventured, nothing gained* - and took the risk to implement this idea.

This approach succeeded, accelerating installation of the new computer system by about two years and saving over $1 million in development costs. This innovative approach became a model for risk-taking and value partnering between functions.

Application in Education

A team of educators in southern Delaware sponsored a seminar for a graduating class of about 100 high school students with the objective of introducing them to creative thinking skills. To illustrate the process and capture their attention, this needs-driven issue was selected:

> *How can we make learning in the classroom more fun?*

The first step was to explain lateral thinking, followed by audience participation to apply this technique to the problem. All students participated by interacting with their neighbors. A group of six volunteers was situated at a table up front that was equipped with loudspeakers. Many provocations were developed using lateral thinking.

Wishful thinking led to this provocation:

Eliminate teachers.

This provocation triggered the idea that once a month the teacher would become part of the student group and a student or team of students would take turns conducting the lesson. Several teachers in the audience said they would seriously consider implementing this idea.

Speed of Delivery of a New Innovation

This example illustrates how lateral thinking was applied to generate an idea for commercializing a new nylon product in record time.

A research an development unit had made a technical breakthrough that would enable economic manufacture of a proprietary new product innovation. This was a high-priority program. The organization was anxious to move this product to market much faster than the normal development cycle. A cross-functional team applied lateral thinking to address this needs-driven issue:

How can we move the new product to market faster?

The provocation technique that paid off in this instance was *random word*. The random word was *beach*, selected from a billboard bathing suit advertisement. Thinking about *beach* led to a series of thoughts relating to water, to swimming, to swim meets and to competition. The thought of competition triggered this provocation:

Give the breakthrough technology to our toughest competitor.

This was certainly provocative! It triggered thinking about who was the toughest competitor and how they would bring this breakthrough to market. The toughest competitor in this case was a Japanese company known to move new products to market rapidly.

Questioning how the competitor would handle this breakthrough led to an idea about an organizational structure quite different from the prevailing DuPont culture. The idea was accepted by marketing, engineering, manufacturing, and business functions after much discussion, despite some difficult turf issues. The product was introduced two to three years faster than normal. This saved millions of dollars in development costs and enabled early assessment of the new product innovation in the marketplace.

Growing a Business

This example illustrates how lateral thinking and metaphoric thinking generated unusual ideas to aid in meeting a need to grow a business faster.

A business unit had commercialized a new plant in Europe and therefore had much higher capacity than it had sales. There was an urgent need to take steps to increase sales. The business director was familiar with the problem-solving process and requested his strategic planning team to organize a session to address the needs-driven issue:

How can we grow our business faster?

A multifunctional team consisting of marketing, technical, manufacturing, strategic business planners, and two "wild cards" was convened. A "wild card" is a person known to be a creative thinker, but who is unfamiliar with the issue being addressed. Hence, the "wild card" brings a fresh point of view.

Most of the participants had attended creative thinking seminars and workshops, and were eager to apply their knowledge to a high-stakes, practical issue. Facilitators trained in problem-solving and creative thinking techniques were enlisted to lead the session.

Lateral thinking and metaphoric thinking paid off, yielding many unusual ideas judged to be of value.

Lateral thinking generated this provocation:

Don't sell the product.

This led to the concept of leasing the product. This was feasible for many of the products in this particular business. This idea would likely never have been thought of using normal thinking patterns.

Metaphoric thinking, which will be discussed later in this section, led to this question:

How are trees and shrubs grown?

This thought led to the concept of "pruning." The idea was to "prune" customers that were forecast to have low growth rates. This would free up technical service and marketing resources to grow the business faster by better servicing customers forecast to have high growth rate.

Metaphoric Thinking

Metaphoric thinking is another powerful creative thinking technique. It involves searching for systems or problems that are unrelated, but in some ways similar to the problem under attack. The challenge is to understand how the problem was solved in the other system, which often leads to new ideas about the one under attack.

Sometimes, understanding how nature solved a related problem yields many useful ideas. Dr. Jonas Salk once commented:

I try to think like nature to find the right questions. You don't invent the answers, you reveal the answers from nature. In nature the answers to our problems already exist Ask how nature would solve this problem.

Described below are two examples where metaphoric thinking was successfully applied.

"Nomex Colorguard"

This example describes how a researcher, who had attended creativity seminars, applied metaphoric thinking to solve a difficult technical problem. His creative thinking led to an important new product innovation.

"Nomex" aramid fiber is an inherently flame resistant fiber which is used in protective clothing, electrical insulation, and honeycomb aircraft panels. To expand Nomex markets into flame-resistant fabrics for drapes, upholstery, and carpets, a need existed to develop a product that could be dyed in customers' mills without special procedures. Because the fiber had a very tight structure, the dyeing process required swelling agents that were costly and caused environmental problems. Many research programs failed to accomplish the objective of a readily dyeable Nomex.

Eric Vance, an innovative research scientist working on the Nomex dyeing problem, attended creativity seminars that described many creative thinking techniques, including metaphoric thinking. He applied this technique to the problem. He asked himself:

What in nature has a tight structure, but can be penetrated - and how?

His answer:

The earth! - Coal miners gain access to the interior of the earth by digging holes and propping them open.

Inspired by this metaphor, Vance added a large organic molecule into the fiber structure during manufacture to prop open the structure of the forming Nomex fiber. This allowed entrance of dyes under standard mill conditions. The dye entered, the props collapsed, and the dyes stayed in the fiber.

A dyeable, flame-resistant Nomex, trademarked Colorguard®, was commercialized, opening up many potential new applications for Nomex in colorful, flame retardant upholstery, drapes and carpets.

Dust Reduction

This example illustrates how metaphoric thinking stimulated ideas to meet the need for an innovative way to reduce copious amounts of dust in a plant.

A manufacturing team was dealing with serious cost and quality problems across the plant caused by dust generated in one of their processes. They had developed a long list of ideas to reduce the dust, but none were very good. Several members of the team had attended creative thinking workshops and suggested a creative thinking session to attack this needs-driven problem:

How can we reduce dust in our plant?

The technique that paid off was metaphoric thinking. They questioned:

How does nature remove dust from the environment?

They reasoned that one way that nature removes dust from the environment is by heavy rainfall. This thought shifted their thinking to an entirely new direction that led to an elegant but simple way to remove dust in their plant operation.

Capturing & Interpreting Dreams

Capturing and interpreting dreams is a Ned Herrmann creativity technique involving harnessing of the subconscious. It's a way to seed new ideas, solve problems, and envision new opportunities.

Have you ever experienced going to sleep with a problem and waking up the next morning with a clearer view of the problem and new approaches to solving it? This happens because the mind continues to function while we sleep. In the subconscious state, the mind is less inhibited.

The *Applied Creative Thinking* workshop sponsored by Ned Herrmann, teaches keeping a pad and pen at bedside to record dreams immediately after awakening. Otherwise dreams are quickly forgotten. Once in hand, dreams can be interpreted relative to the problem on the person's mind the night before, as illustrated in the example described below.

Collapsing Vacuum Hose

This example illustrates how a dream helped meet a need to creatively solve a difficult plant process problem that was taking a serious, costly toll on yields.

The "creative dreamer" was Floyd Ragsdale, an innovator in the Kevlar plant who had participated in on-site creativity workshops. Manufacturing was dealing with a process problem that was causing quality and cost problems. His account of the problem and creative solution follows:

We had been fighting collapsing vacuum hoses in the Kevlar process for months. It was taking a tremendous toll on our yields. One day, I had been at the plant trying to find a solution for maybe 16 hours, and I needed some sleep. When I went home and got to bed ,the problem throbbed in my head like a toothache, back and forth, back and forth.

Eventually, I fell asleep. I started to dream, and in my dreams, I saw slinky toys, those spring-like coils that kids play with. I kept seeing these toy-like springs, over and over. I had been to a creativity workshop at the plant only a month before. One of the lessons was that we should pay attention to our dreams, because sometimes we have better insights when we relax and don't concentrate so hard. So I kept a pad and paper next to my bed. I came out of my dream and sat up. Still half asleep, I wrote on my pad:

"Insert spring inside of vacuum hose, will correct problem."

Then I went back to sleep.

When I woke up at about 4:30 or 5:00 and headed into the plant, I took my paper with me. I saw the area supervisor and said, "We're in luck. I had a dream. Our problem is solved." He looked at me kind of funny, but I explained, and we ordered some customized stainless steel springs and inserted them in the hose. Doggone, that equipment started up running like a top and has been running well ever since.

Some people may wonder why the plant team had not thought about a spring sooner, it seemed so obvious. But most good ideas are obvious in hindsight. How often has someone come up with a good idea and you wondered why that hadn't been thought of before? It's like climbing a mountain and not seeing the best path up until reaching the top and looking down. It seems obvious in hindsight, but it wasn't apparent while "climbing that mountain."

Challenging Conventional Wisdom

Tom Alexander, in his book *The Wild Birds Find a Corporate Roost* writes:

When a distinguished, but elderly scientist states that something is possible, he is almost always certainly right. When he states that something is impossible, he is very probably wrong.

Challenging conventional wisdom is the deliberate questioning of existing paradigms and a willingness to take risks to buck the tide of popular opinion. This characteristic comes naturally to many outstanding scientific researchers.

The DuPont Pioneering Research Laboratory fostered an environment for thinking positively and questioning conventional wisdom. This was a vital factor repeatedly in the successful development and commercialization of the "Kevlar" innovation described in Chapter XI.

Point of View

Challenging our "point of view" about an issue, an event, or a thing can jog our thinking outside normal patterns and can lead to entirely new ideas and concepts.

A technique taught by Roger von Oech is to substitute your own thinking with the point of view of another person known for having a unique style of creative thinking (Ref. 30). The example described below illustrates the application of this technique.

Cutting Through Red Tape

A business team was searching for needs-driven ideas on how to commercialize a product rapidly by cutting through administrative red tape. The technique that proved the most useful in this case was to view the problem from the point of view of Lee Iacocca.

Someone in the group related a story he had heard about how Lee Iacocca re-entered Chrysler into the convertible automobile market. At the time, convertibles had been out of style for years because of safety issues. Iacocca decided to test the public reaction to a convertible and asked his manufacturing manager how fast he could deliver a convertible to display. The response was that if given high priority, it could be ready in six months.

As the story goes, Iacocca turned red with anger. He ordered the manager to rip off the roof of an existing car and have the convertible ready by the next morning.

The above story lifted the business team to a more intensive plateau of creative thinking. There was a burst of aggressive, unorthodox ideas in tune with how Iacocca would address their problem, e.g., elimination of all paperwork. This session paid off and helped lay the basis of a fast-track program.

Dare to be Different

Mike Emery, Business Director at "Tyvek" , promoted this point of view:

Dare to be Different.

His concept was that innovators would benefit by willing to be different in a positive, constructive way. The only constraints were that the action be legal, moral, and safe. An example that illustrates his approach and willingness to *practice what he preached* is described below.

A marketing rep in Emery's organization visited a customer to react to a complaint. The rep concluded that the complaint was valid. He took out his wallet and paid the claim. He charged it on his expense account. The company accountants yelled "foul." Emery had a party to acknowledge the marketing rep's *daring to be different*, giving status to this act and reinforcing the environment for creative thinking.

Fantasizing

A technique taught by Joyce Juntune and Morris Stein is to change your point of view about an object by first eyeing it analytically and then fantasizing.

For example, select a pencil and describe it from an analytical point of view. It might be round, yellow, eight inches long, have a grey lead point and a half-worn eraser. Now fantasize. I wish the pencil could do the following: write by itself; be eaten; never wear out; sharpen itself; write in several colors; and illuminate the darkness.

Using this technique with a team of three or four innovative thinkers would likely generate, within 30 minutes, over 100 ideas from which some could be selected to form the basis for a new line of pencils.

Capitalizing on the "Unexpected"

Unexpected results sometimes occur that are ignored as a mistake or failure. At other times, innovators with a "prepared" mind recognize that the unexpected happening might present an opportunity for an important innovation.

Reprinted with permission, Frank and Ernest Cartoons ccThaves

This section describes two product innovations sparked by capitalizing on the unexpected.

Spunbonded Nonwoven Fabrics

This example illustrates how a major new business venture was born by a research engineer observing an unusual phenomenon that he associated with a need, triggering an idea to meet the need.

A research engineer at the DuPont Carothers Research Laboratory was exploring ways to spin a fuzzy nylon filament yarn. His approach was to blow short floc fibers against a molten spinning threadline to obtain hair-like projections. He couldn't get the floc fibers to stick, so he tried electrostatics. Normally the yarn is wound up on a bobbin, but the spinning operator was late in inserting the windup bobbin. Therefore, the yarn fell to the floor. As it did so, the electro-statically charged fibers spread out into a sheet-like structure.

At the time, the mid-1950s, there was a need in the marketplace for low-cost nonwoven fabrics from synthetic fibers. The engineer was aware of this need. When he observed the fibers spreading into sheet structures on the floor, he realized that this was an entirely new concept in sheet structure formation. This observation ultimately led to DuPont's Reemay® and Typar® spunbonded, nonwoven fabric innovations.

Dye-Resistant New Styling Yarns

This example illustrates how a positive-thinking innovator interpreted an unexpected negative result in a positive way, resulting in a valuable new product innovation.

A need existed for a more rapidly dyeable nylon carpet fiber. A research scientist took the approach to chemically modify the nylon polymer. In one experiment, the result was the opposite of what he expected or wanted. The fiber could not be dyed at all! Instead of discarding this negative result, he took a positive view. He reasoned that he could mix this non-dyeable fiber with dyeable fibers and get unique styling effects. This was the birth of dye-resist styling yarns, which materialized into a profitable product in the nylon carpet line.

Idea Collection Processes

There are many processes that help collect and organize ideas generated within normal thinking patterns. In problem-solving sessions, it is best to start with some of these processes. When teams have exhausted ideas generated within normal thinking patterns, then pattern-breaking techniques such as lateral thinking and metaphoric thinking, discussed in the previous section, help trigger a flow of new, more unusual creative ideas. This section reviews some idea-collection processes:

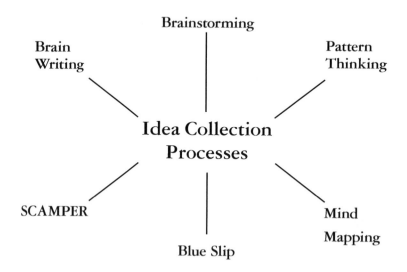

Brainstorming

In 1938, Alex Osborne first employed organized ideation in the company he then headed (Ref. 6, 7). The early participants dubbed their efforts "Brainstorm Sessions", because they were using their brains to storm a problem. Brainstorming became popular worldwide. It is defined in Merriam Webster's Collegiate Dictionary, 10th Edition, as:

> *A group problem-solving technique that involves the spontaneous contribution of ideas from all members of the group.*

Osborne points out in his book that this type of session was not entirely new. A similar procedure has been used in India for more than 400 years by Hindu teachers while working with religious groups. The Indian name for this method is Prai-Barshana. In such a session there is no discussion or criticism. Evaluation of ideas take place at later meetings of the same group.

Modern brainstorming is usually part of a problem-solving session in which a checklist of ideas is generated that leads to problem solution. The objective is to collect, usually on hang charts, a large quantity of ideas. Building on others' ideas is encouraged. The deferment-of-judgment principle is strictly followed. The ideas are subsequently evaluated and processed.

Printed with permission, Frank and Ernest Cartoons, ccThaves

A brainstorming warm up helps to create an environment and mind-frame conducive to an uninhibited free-flow of ideas. An effective, challenging technique is for the facilitator to use a five-minute brainstorming exercise that asks teams to think of 50 -100 ideas on how to modify a bathtub. The teams, with some effort, are generally able to do this. Then the facilitator unexpectedly asks teams for an additional 50-100 bathtub ideas, which is more difficult. The teams find, to their surprise, that they are able to do this. By the time the participants complete this exercise, they have lost their mental inhibitions and are ready to brainstorm the problem at hand.

A competent facilitator, knowledgeable about how to conduct a process for evaluating and harvesting best ideas, is required to have an effective problem-solving session.

An example where brainstorming was successfully applied to solve a problem is described in The "Honey-Pot" Story, related in Chapter II.

While brainstorming is the most well-known technique for generating ideas in problem-solving, our experience over the years has been that there are more powerful, productive techniques for generating "out-of-the -box" ideas. In fact Susan Cain, in her new book *Quiet : The Power of Introverts in a World That Can't Stop Talking* (Ref. 48), asserted that brainstorming isn't the golden ticket to innovation after all, that groups are not necessarily more creative than individuals, and that brainstorming can actually be detrimental to good ideas. The earlier section on pattern-breaking tools describes some other idea-generating techniques including lateral thinking and metaphoric thinking.

Pattern Thinking

Pattern thinking is the most basic of the idea-collection processes. It involves bringing to bear a person's best thinking on how to solve a problem based on his or her knowledge and experience. It differs from brainstorming in that the focus in pattern thinking is on quality rather than quantity.

Pattern thinking is a good way to begin the idea generation step in a creative problem-solving session. It enables participants to air their best ideas in a focused way to solve the problem within their normal experience base. As in brainstorming, building on others' ideas is encouraged. After pattern thinking, the facilitator generally employs other idea-generating methods such as those described in the section describing pattern-breaking tools.

All ideas are captured on hang charts as part of the total pool of ideas collected during the session. In harvesting best ideas, some that were collected during pattern thinking are often among the best ideas considered for action planning.

Mind Mapping

Mind mapping is a process originated by Tony Buzon that combines right-brain generation of ideas with left-brain organization of those ideas around a central theme. In contrast with traditional listing of ideas or thoughts down a page, mind mapping places the core subject in the center of the page as a starting point for the generation of multiple ideas that branch out in many directions. Mind mapping has many applications, including note-taking, organizing presentations, and problem-solving. It is a productive aid to group or individual brainstorming.

Mind mapping laws, including the use of color and images, are listed in Buzon's book (Ref. 19). In practice, there are many variations depending on individual preferences. Joyce Wycoff's workbook provides an excellent overview of mind mapping and approach to practical applications (Ref. 20).

A mind map helped to organize this chapter:

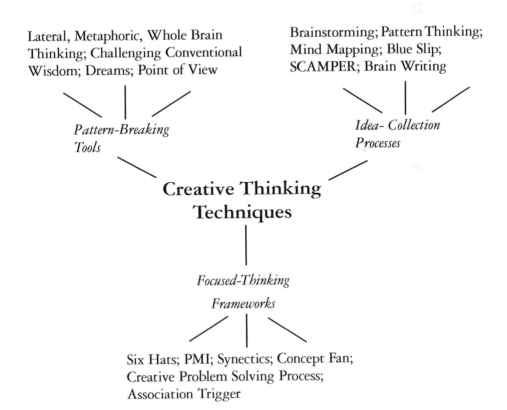

Lateral, Metaphoric, Whole Brain Thinking; Challenging Conventional Wisdom; Dreams; Point of View

Brainstorming; Pattern Thinking; Mind Mapping; Blue Slip; SCAMPER; Brain Writing

Pattern-Breaking Tools

Idea- Collection Processes

Creative Thinking Techniques

Focused-Thinking

Frameworks

Six Hats; PMI; Synectics; Concept Fan; Creative Problem Solving Process; Association Trigger

Blue Slip

The blue slip process has been taught by Rolf Smith and Dale Clawson, former directors, Office of Innovation, United States Air Force. The technique involves writing ideas on 4" x 3" blue slips, usually in response to a thought-provoking question. Each slip has a subject title at the top and one idea..

The blue slip process is an excellent way to collect and assemble ideas generated in a group discussion, and to record and save one's own ideas on an ongoing basis.

As an example of practical application, the blue slip process was applied in a meeting of technical managers to identify ways to improve functional effectiveness. Four questions asked by Colonel Rolf Smith:

- If you could be in charge for a year, what would you change?

- What prevents you from doing your job better?

- What can we stop doing?

- What should we not tamper with?

Participants wrote down their thoughts on many blue slips as each question was asked. The slips were collected and summarized, and the ideas were used as a basis for discussion at the next technical function meeting, where an action plan was formulated.

SCAMPER

This technique, developed by Bob Eberle, (Ref. 21) provides a checklist acronym of seven verbs to systematically stimulate ideas: Substitute; Combine; Adapt; Modify; Put to other uses; Eliminate; and Rearrange.

The SCAMPER technique has been used in the classroom by Ronni Cohen, elementary school teacher and winner of the 1994 National

Entrepreneurship Educator of the Year Award, to generate ideas about how to creatively invent new products.

Cohen illustrated practical application of the process in a monthly meeting of the Creative Educator Network of Delaware (page ...). The group of about thirty educators, parents and scientists applied SCAMPER to creatively design a modernistic briefcase for the 21st century. Within 10 minutes, teams developed numerous, unusual concepts for an innovative new briefcase, such as one that can unfold into a backpack when needed.

Brain Writing

This technique has members of a problem-solving team silently build on each others' ideas. It is a way to collect ideas from less vocal team members.

The process starts with one participant listing three ideas related to the problem across the top of a sheet of paper. The sheet of paper is then placed in the center of the table. Another team member picks up this sheet and adds his or her ideas, stimulated by the other persons' ideas. This continues until the sheets of paper are filled. The facilitator then posts these sheets on hang charts for future processing along with other ideas generated during the problem-solving session.

Focused Thinking Frameworks

The quality of our thinking will determine the quality of our future.

- Edward de Bono

Focused thinking frameworks play a vital role in structuring the approach to problem-solving, opportunity-searching, and creatively organizing one's thoughts around a subject or issue. This section describes six productive frameworks for focused thinking:

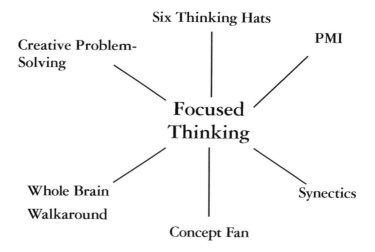

Six Thinking Hats

Creative Problem-
Solving

PMI

**Focused
Thinking**

Whole Brain
Walkaround

Synectics

Concept Fan

The Six Thinking Hats

The Six Thinking Hats, designed by Dr. Edward de Bono, is an ingenious framework to think through a subject in a focused way that makes time and space for creative thinking (Ref. 10). It has been used extensively in companies such as DuPont, IBM, Prudential Life Insurance, British Airways, and Hewlett Packard as a way to have efficient, productive meetings, especially when dealing with complex, controversial issues where emotions run high. This framework is taught in certification courses by de Bono Thinking Systems (Ref. 18).

The underlying principle in the Six Thinking Hats framework is that *parallel thinking* is more productive than argument. The six hats are shown below.

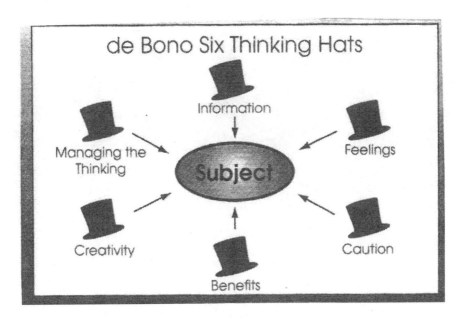

de Bono Six Thinking Hats

Information

Managing the Thinking

Feelings

Subject

Creativity

Benefits

Caution

Reprinted with permission. cc2012. I P Development Corporation
Published by de Bono Thinking Systems

Each hat has a different color and represents a different dimension in thinking about the subject being addressed. The *White Hat* deals with information, the *Red Hat* with feelings, the *Yellow Hat* with benefits, the *Black Hat* with caution, the *Green Hat* with creative ideas, and the *Blue Hat* with thinking about managing the thinking. Everyone wears the same hat at the same time.

Hats can be put on and taken off depending on the sequence in thinking that makes the most sense. It's something like using a set of golf clubs. Each club has a different purpose and can be taken out and put back depending on the situation. Six Thinking Hats can be used individually or in groups, at work or at home. Each hat is described in more detail below.

White Hat Thinking

Think of paper or a computer printout. This hat deals with factual information. What information do we have? What information do we need? It provides background to the issue being addressed. It pinpoints action needed to fill gaps. Importantly, it separates fact from speculation.

FRANK AND ERNEST by Bob Thaves

PERSONNEL

ANY AWARDS OR HONORS FROM ANYBODY OTHER THAN YOUR MOM?

THAVES 9-4

Reprinted with permission, Frank and Ernest Cartoons ccThaves

The following story illustrates White Hat thinking in a humorous way:

A man named Arnold was standing on a street corner with a dog at his side. A second man approaches and asks, "If I pet your dog, will your dog bite me?" Arnold replies, "My dog doesn't bite." So the man pets the dog and the dog bites him! He says, "I thought you said that your dog doesn't bite!" Arnold replies, "This isn't my dog."

Red Hat Thinking

Think of fire or warmth. The *Red Hat* deals with feelings, intuition, and emotions. It gives participants permission to express feelings. There is no need to justify or explain reasons. The *Red Hat* also covers "gut" feelings based on experience. In dealing with important issues at home or at work where a decision is required, we may collect much information related to the issue, but we usually make our final decision based on our "gut" feeling.

The *Red Hat* is often used during a creative thinking session to invite participants to express feelings about whether an idea should be implemented. A business meeting addressing a controversial issue might start out with each person wearing the *Red Hat* to express their feelings about the subject. This sometimes will change the meeting agenda.

Yellow Hat Thinking

Think of sunshine. This is the "positive thinking" hat. It relates to benefits, values, and the feasibility that an idea will work. When wearing this hat everyone thinks positively. *Yellow Hat* thinking reinforces creative ideas and new directions. *Yellow Hat* thinking points need to be supported by logical reasons. Often the *Yellow Hat* is used early in a session to support benefits of an idea or concept. An important value of the *Yellow Hat* is that even people opposed to an idea are forced to think positively and may be stimulated to contribute creative benefits.

Black Hat Thinking

Think of a judge wearing a black robe. This hat deals with judgment, caution, difficulties, and risks. It is a valuable, necessary, and very important hat. It prevents false starts and silly mistakes. It pinpoints weaknesses and impracticalities. Overusing the Black Hat creates a serious problem. Critical thinking about an idea comes very naturally to most people, so it is not uncommon for overuse of the Black Hat negative mode of thinking.

Green Hat Thinking

Think of vegetation, growth, and energy. This is the creative hat, used to generate new ideas and possibilities and to explore alternate courses of action. Wearing the *Green Hat* provides the opportunity to think creatively about how to gain the benefits of a good idea while overcoming barriers. *Green Hat* thinking is catalyzed by creativity tools such as lateral thinking.

Blue Hat Thinking

Think of a blue sky or an overview. This hat manages the thinking process. When participants wear the *Blue Hat*, they are thinking about thinking, e.g., what sequence of hats makes most sense in dealing with the issue. This hat is also involved with process control. The person leading the session often has to remind people which hat is being worn. When the group is wearing the *Yellow Hat*, some folks might find it tempting to be critical of a benefit. The leader would then suggest postponing the criticism until the group wears the *Black Hat*. The *Blue Hat* is also worn when it is time to summarize output of the meeting.

Summary of the Focused-Thinking Framework

The Six Thinking Hats framework:

- Encourages parallel thinking with others,

- Directs thinking in discreet segments,

- Switches thinking from one mode to another,

- Explores a subject more thoroughly,

- Makes specific time and space for creative thinking,

- Separates ego from performance, and

- Can be used individually or in groups.

This has been a brief description of the Six Thinking Hats.

Workshops are available to learn and practice this valuable framework in depth (Ref.18). When dealing with an important issue impacting an organization, it's essential that an experienced facilitator lead the process.

Applications

The Six Hats Framework can be used in a variety of ways:

- Evaluating and upgrading ideas and proposals,

- Planning for implementation of an innovative idea,

- Resolving controversial issues, and

- Generating new ideas and concepts.

Resolving Controversial Issues

This example describes how the Six Thinking Hats framework helped settle a controversial technical issue that had stymied progress in development of a major new product innovation.

A West Coast high-technology company embarked upon an effort to develop a next-generation, bread-and-butter product. An engineering task force was formed that spent several weeks identifying three alternative approaches. However, progress was stymied because of disagreement on which of the three approaches to pursue. They badly needed to resolve this issue for the program to proceed.

The task-force leader was familiar with the creative thinking field and hired an experienced facilitator to help resolve this problem. The Six

Thinking Hats framework was ideal to lead the team through a focused thinking session to evaluate and upgrade each approach.

As a first step, the Six Thinking Hats framework was reviewed. The team was then divided into three subgroups, each applying the Six Hats framework to evaluate and upgrade one of the three next-generation approaches.

Each team started with *Yellow Hat* thinking to define benefits and feasibility. *Black Hat* thinking defined barriers. *Green Hat* thinking generated creative ideas on how to overcome barriers, retain benefits, and upgrade the technical approach. *White Hat* thinking identified information needed to fill gaps in their knowledge.

At several points in the session, each team shared its Six Thinking Hats thinking with the entire group to benefit from each others' views. Particularly productive was the sharing of *Green Hat* ideas on ways to upgrade the technical concepts of each approach.

During the final hour of the session, *Red Hat* thinking gave participants the opportunity to share their feelings on which approach was best. Having thought through the issue in a focused way, there was a unanimous agreement on which path had the most promise. An important benefit of this session was buy-in by all team members on which was the best path to pursue.

Focused Thinking About a Family Issue

A young student graduating from college as a finance major decided that, instead of looking for a job, he wanted to start his own business. He asked his father for financial support to purchase a franchise. The father suggested thinking about this project using the Six Thinking Hats framework, which both of them were already familiar with.

Using the White Hat, the son described information he had about the franchise. At this time his father asked many questions to better understand the background and potential opportunity. Using Yellow Hat thinking, the son made many positive points about the franchise benefits. As the father became acquainted with the prospects, he enthusiastically joined the son in listing potential benefits. During Black Hat thinking, the mother became a valued member of the team. This was beneficial to the process, since critical thinking came easily for her.

In this session, White Hat thinking was quite valuable. Toward the end of the discussion, the family put the white thinking hat back on and focused in parallel on what additional information would be needed before a decision would be made. This became the basis for action steps. Guess what the family used as the focal point in their Green Hat thinking: *What alternatives are available to finance the venture?*

The entire session took close to an hour to think through the proposal, generate action steps, and gain the buy-in of all concerned. The outcome was that the father did finance the project which turned out to be very successful. The son paid back the fathers the loan within one year.

Evaluating and Upgrading Ideas

This example describes how the Six Thinking Hats framework helped evaluate a controversial idea aimed at developing a portfolio of new products.

An R&D planning team of the DuPont Industrial Products Division recommended to divisional management the formation of a new business that would capitalize on the combined strengths of the existing individual businesses of Kevlar®, Nomex®, Tyvek®, Sontara®, and Teflon®.

The idea was controversial. Business managers felt it would dilute resources from their businesses and were strongly opposed. R&D management was strongly in favor. A two-hour meeting was scheduled to evaluate this controversial idea. The meeting was designed based on the Six Thinking Hats framework. The business managers were agreeable since the division had an ongoing creative thinking program, and they were familiar with the value of this framework. The divisional facilitator led the session, supported by the divisional Creativity Manager.

The meeting started with a brief *White Hat* overview and discussion of the proposed idea. Then, instead of *Yellow Hat* thinking to elicit positive benefits, which is the usual sequence of hats, the facilitator initiated *Black Hat* thinking. An energetic discussion by business managers resulted in many hang charts listing serious difficulties with the idea. This allowed business managers to air reasons, many justified, why they were opposed.

Next they used *Yellow Hat* thinking. In the beginning there was dead silence. The R&D people purposely said nothing. Then, Chad Holliday, one of the business managers noted a benefit. This started the ball rolling. Soon, all business managers joined in, and there were as many hang charts of the benefits as those containing difficulties.

Green Hat thinking generated many creative ideas on how to retain benefits while overcoming difficulties. Everyone was now energetically engaged in upgrading the idea to make it workable. The R&D planning team was charged to develop a stepwise implementation plan for further review, embodying the suggested changes. The business managers now had strong buy-in.

In subsequent meetings, agreement was reached on next steps. Many years later, a DuPont Safety & Protection business segment was formed, which embodies many of the principles discussed in the Six Thinking Hats session.

Dealing with an Education Issue

David Campbell, a District Superintendant in the Delaware school system, invited a DuPont-trained problem-solving facilitator to attend a monthly meeting of the six North Delaware School Superintendants to discuss the potential application of creative thinking knowledge in the education system.

At one of the monthly meetings, the facilitator asked each superintendent to write down the three most important issues they were personally dealing with. This caught their attention! As they each volunteered their issues, the issues were listed on the blackboard. After eliminating duplications, there were eight issues of primary interest. These were discussed, and they agreed that the most important issue pertinent to all of them was:

> *How can we achieve third-grade reading competencies for all students upon completion of third grade?*

They were all anxious to tackle this issue and agreed to schedule a half-day creative thinking session. For this session, each superintendant agreed to bring with them three educators, including principals from their respective school districts.

The half-day meeting was held to deal with the above issue, led by two experienced facilitators from the DuPont Center for Creativity & Innovation.

The group of 30 participants generated numerous ideas related to this issue, using various creativity tools. Convergent thinking led to selection of the three best ideas. The Six Thinking Hats framework was then applied to evaluate and upgrade these three ideas.

Each team shared their thinking with the whole group who then voted on the best idea to consider implementing. The selected idea:

Teach parents how to teach reading in the home.

The concept was that most parents play a key role in teaching their children how to talk, how to walk, and how to ride a bicycle. Why not teach parents how to teach children how to read? Some of the participants were enthused about pursuing this idea.

At a later date, a DuPont facilitator was invited by a professor from Drexel University in Philadelphia, to introduce her class of Ph.D. candidates in education, to the creativity and innovation field. As part of the lecture, the class was introduced to the Six Thinking Hats.

To illustrate the practical value of this framework, the class of about 20 students was asked to evaluate the idea generated by the Delaware District Superintendant's meeting described above. The Six Thinking Hats approach allowed them to evaluate the idea in a focused way, but with intense differences of opinion while wearing the *Yellow* and *Black* hats multiple times and periodically putting on the *Green* hat.

The scheduled one-hour evening class lasted over three hours without gaining unanimous agreement on whether this was a good idea for the education community to pursue. However, the professor later commented that many of her students were so impacted by the Six Thinking Hats process, that it completely changed their approach to dealing with issues.

Reversing Opinion on an Important Proposal

The following example describes how a corporate team applied the Six Thinking Hat process to address the need to resolve a controversial proposal with important budget control implications. The result was to reverse initial thinking about the proposed idea.

A corporate advisory team of eight high level members was formed to deal with an idea that had emerged from an executive strategic planning meeting. The idea was that all R&D Directors in the company should submit a structured cost-benefit analysis on each of their major programs to help decide annual budget allocations.

Corporate team members looked favorably on the proposed idea and felt it should be implemented. R&D Directors were strongly opposed, concerned that the implications had not been thought through carefully enough.

A one-hour meeting was organized to resolve this controversial proposal. The group was familiar with the Six Thinking Hats process because of a corporate creativity and innovation program and decided to apply this framework to accomplish the task. An experienced facilitator from the DuPont Center for Creativity & Innovation was assigned to lead the session. He was delighted as he had been practicing the Six Thinking Hats framework for several weeks since taking a training workshop. Now was his chance to apply his learnings to an important issue.

The meeting began with a brief review of the Six Thinking Hats. *White Hat* thinking provided time for discussion of the proposed idea. *Yellow Hat* thinking generated a long list of benefits. It appeared obvious that the idea should be implemented. However, it turned out to be otherwise. In *Black Hat* thinking many serious negatives emerged, such as the credibility of cost-benefit assumptions. *Green Hat* thinking generated creative ideas for upgrading the idea to overcome obstacles, but none of the ideas was convincing. *Red Hat* thinking enabled each participant to express feelings about the proposal. The corporate advisory team reversed their original thinking and decided against the proposal.

Harvesting Best Ideas

The next example illustrates how the Six Thinking Hats process helped a food company harvest their best ideas for dealing with the need to increase the speed of delivery of their product. It illustrates the step-wise process of applying the Six Thinking Hats to think through a practical opportunity.

The manager of a mid-western food company, familiar with the creative thinking field organized a session to develop ideas on how to improve competitive position in home delivery of the company's food products. An experienced facilitator led the meeting attended by a team of twelve participants who generated many ideas using several creative thinking techniques. The ideas were posted on flip charts. From this list, the group selected the three ideas they perceived to be the best for further evaluation and upgrading.

The final step was to harvest the best of these three ideas. The Six Thinking Hats provided a framework to think through each of the selected ideas in a focused way. The sequence began with *Yellow Hat* thinking to define benefits that helped reinforce the idea. *Black Hat* thinking focused attention on difficulties and barriers that would have to be overcome. *Green Hat* thinking led to creative ways to overcome barriers while maintaining benefits. *White Hat* thinking identified information needed to fill gaps in the knowledge base and to implement the idea.

This sequence was followed for each of the three ideas, enabling the team to gain a better understanding of each idea. Finally, each participant used the *Red Hat* to express their feelings about which ideas to implement.

This two-hour session provided the manager with three well thought-out ideas to increase competitive position and helped him decide which one to pursue. Another benefit was team buy-in of the idea selected for implementation.

PMI

The PMI is an Edward de Bono focused thinking model for treatment of ideas where:

"P" stands for what's **Plus** about the idea, i.e., the good points.

"M" stands for what's **Minus** about the idea, i.e., the bad points.

"I" stands for what's **Interesting** about the idea, i.e., points that are neither good nor bad, but are worth noting.

The PMI is the first lesson of the de Bono CoRT thinking lessons being widely used in schools for the direct teaching of thinking as a basic skill (Ref. 22). The PMI is a useful framework to get rapid feed-back on an idea. It helps bypass people's natural emotional reaction to an idea.

The following example illustrates the value of the PMI.

A motivational video was being prepared for a major DuPont conference to illustrate the value of day-to-day ideas in the innovation process. The video was in draft form and ready for critical review prior to finalizing. That week, there was a new employee orientation program with a one-hour session scheduled for a facilitator to introduce the field of creative thinking. This provided an opportunity to teach the PMI to the 30 participants and concurrently apply it to a practical issue, namely to critique the proposed video.

The PMI framework was explained and the video was then shown. Within about 20 minutes, the group learned the PMI and applied it to the video. This session provided constructive input that led to a much-improved video. For example, some of the minus points were that it was too long, and the narrator was too "professional", which gave the impression of a TV commercial. Some of the plus points were the basic message and the lively music. Some of the interesting points related to the general flow and visual effects.

Synectics

The co-developer of the Synectics framework, George M. Prince made this comment:

> *The Synectics system has been called by some as an artificial vacation, because it seems to let us take a holiday from the problem by not having to think about it consciously for awhile, and it encouraged us to put aside our business-suit thinking, our usual tight, analytical frame of mind ; but it is an artificial vacation, because while our conscious mind is making the analogies, our preconscious is hard at work on the problem.*

Synectics is a problem-solving framework developed by W. J. J. Gordon and George M. Prince that uses a multi-step process including metaphoric thinking as the main creative thinking tool (Ref.24). This framework has the following basic steps:

1. **The problem (or opportunity)as given** - This is the problem statement to be attacked. Analysis in Synectics is explanation of the problem by the expert (owner of the problem).

2. **Goals as Understood** - This step identifies possible focus areas where the group uses the technique of wishful thinking. It helps break complex problems into manageable parts. The client selects the focus area to work on.

3. **Mental Excursion** - This step involves "taking a vacation from the problem" using several approaches to metaphoric thinking. For example, the leader challenges participants to think of examples of phenomena that are similar to the subject at hand. He or she then chooses an example that is interesting, strange or irrelevant to the problem.

4. **Force Fit** - This is considered the most difficult step in the Synectics procedure. This is where the metaphorical material must be forced to be useful, even if it seems irrelevant to the problem. It is the point in the process for generating breakthrough ideas relevant to solving the problem. Prince uses the stories of Archemedes in the bathtub and Isaac Newton's experience beneath the apple tree to illustrate how an irrelevant stimulus can provide a flash of inspiration.

5. **Viewpoint** - This is the step where possible solutions to the problem are selected for pursuing. Before an idea is accepted as a viewpoint, it must satisfy these two criteria:

- The expert (problem owner) must believe that the idea has new elements and is promising;

- The expert must know exactly what next steps to take to test its validity.

A session is considered successful if the expert has at least five viewpoints to act on.

Many practical examples illustrating the Synectics step-wise process are described in the book *Synectics* (Ref.23).

This process was applied at DuPont to tackle various manufacturing problems such as: How can we increase uniformity of fiber finish application? And how can we reduce streaks produced from bulked continuous filament nylon?

A very-well-trained facilitator, experienced in the Synectics process is required to have a productive problem-solving session using this technique.

Concept Fan

The concept fan is a de Bono technique in which the stated task/issue fans out in broad directions leading to concepts on how to deal with the task, providing several actionable ideas.

For example, in a 1990 meeting of the de Bono International Creative Forum, company representatives were dealing with this issue:

How can we meet the needs of our customers in the year 2000?

It was assumed that the 1990 customer would be ten years old in 2,000. Hence, the task was defined as follows:

How can we access ten-year-olds?

The concept fan was as follows:

Concept Fan

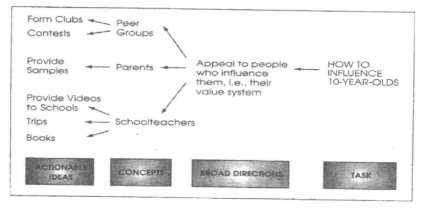

Whole Brain Walkaround

A new perspective about a problem might be gained by viewing it from the four thinking modes of the Ned Herrman whole brain model, described in Chapter VIII, *Diversity in Thinking*.

The whole brain model integrates the scientific study of the brain with the study of creative human development. The basic concept is that the brain is composed of four interactive quadrants, each representing a different category of preferences. The four quadrants:

- The upper left quadrant is better at performing analytical, logical, and mathematical activities.

- The upper right quadrant is better at imaginative, intuitive, and risky activities and tasks.

- The lower left quadrant is prone to structured, sequential and organized mental activities.

- The lower right quadrant is prone to emotional, interpersonal mental activities.

A new perspective about a problem might be gained by an individual or team asking "How would my problem be viewed with sequential focus on each of the quadrants?"

"Walking around" the problem might provide new insights toward a solution. The framework:

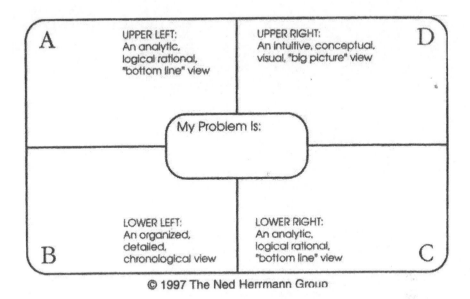

UPPER LEFT:
An analytic,
logical rational,
"bottom line" view

UPPER RIGHT:
An intuitive, conceptual,
visual, "big picture" view

A

D

My Problem Is:

LOWER LEFT:
An organized,
detailed,
chronological view

LOWER RIGHT:
An analytic,
logical rational,
"bottom line" view

B

C

© 1997 The Ned Herrmann Group

The 4-Quadrant Graphic is a registered trademark and copyright of HerrmannGlobal, LLC, and s reproduced with written permission for display in this text.
Copyright 2012 Herrmann Global, LLC. All rights reserved.

The following example illustrates how the problem-solving walkaround was applied to tackle a corporate issue.

One of the themes in a DuPont company world-wide leadership meeting with 400 attendees, was the importance of diversity in achieving the corporate vision. Ned Herrmann was invited to deliver a keynote address outlining brain dominance theory and provided feedback on the HBDI that all participants had taken prior to the meeting.

To illustrate the value of brain dominance theory in problem-solving, a two hour session for a portion of the audience was held using the problem-solving walk-around. This framework was structured with a set of questions in each quadrant designed to stimulate whole-brain thinking on the central issue of *How to Educate DuPonters about the value of creativity and innovation?* - as shown below:

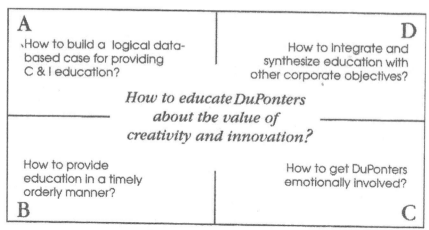

A	D
How to build a logical data-based case for providing C & I education?	How to integrate and synthesize education with other corporate objectives?

How to educate DuPonters about the value of creativity and innovation?

How to provide education in a timely orderly manner?	How to get DuPonters emotionally involved?
B	C

The outcome was a series of ideas that were helpful in accomplishing the stated goal.

Creative Problem-Solving

The creative problem-solving process provides an excellent focused thinking framework to tackle difficult issues. A productive three-step process is described in the next chapter.

VII.

CREATIVE PROBLEM-SOLVING

Many processes for creative problem-solving are described in the literature (Ref. 25). Pioneers at the State University College at Buffalo have published extensively. When the DuPont Center for Creative Thinking & Innovation, described in Chapter X, was formed, several problem-solving processes were benchmarked. Experienced facilitators selected for their workshops the elements from the benchmarked processes that they felt most comfortable with and best suited to meet the needs of the client.

Problem-Solving Process

There are two types of creative problem-solving sessions. In one type, the problem statement is specific enough that the team can delve directly into generating and harvesting ideas. These sessions usually take one to three hours. In the other type of session, the problem statement is so broad that steps are required to define meaningful focus areas. This type often requires a design meeting in advance of the session and time devoted to defining focus areas. The length of these meetings might vary from one to three days. Both types of sessions employ similar techniques in idea generation, harvesting, and implementation planning.

Well-Defined Problems

These sessions begin by stating and discussing a well defined focus area'
e.g.,:

> *- How can we reduce costs in our information systems function?*

> *- How can we reduce dust in our plant?*

> *- How can we make learning in the classroom more fun?*

The creative juices flowed, as the team generated many ideas related to
the stated focus area. It's best to start with team members expressing ideas
within normal thinking patterns. This has the benefit of collecting good
ideas that people may have brought to the meeting. It's a good warm-up.
When the flow of ideas is exhausted using normal thinking patterns, the
facilitator reviews creative thinking techniques.

Facilitators have different preferences regarding the tools they find most
effective and feel comfortable facilitating. The objective is to stir up a new
round of idea generation. Each team member can write his or her ideas
on 3" x 5" Post-it ® notes, read the ideas out loud to help trigger other
people's ideas, and hand the notes to the facilitator for posting on a hang
chart. Individual thinking, followed by sharing of ideas, motivates everyone to participate.

Less Well-Defined Problems

Some problems are stated in less specific terms, i.e.,:

> *- How can we grow our business faster?*

> *- How can we reduce waste in our plants?*

> *- How can we aid business survival?*

While well-defined problems can be addressed in 1–3 hours, less well-defined problems usually require one or more days.

In all creative problem-solving sessions it is important to pay attention to the following components:

Design Meeting

The success of a creative problem-solving session will depend on the quality of the design meeting. The client who initiated the project, a facilitator, and a few other critical people should attend the meeting. A key outcome is to agree on participants, potential focus areas, and the problem statement.

Sometimes, discussion of the original problem statement will lead to a basic change. For example, a manufacturing director originally convened a design meeting with the problem statement:

How can we reduce costs in our plant?

Discussion led to a different problem statement:

How can we make our plant more profitable?

This change broadened the scope of the creative problem-solving session.

Another purpose of the design meeting is to agree on logistics such as length, number of participants, location, and dates. The design meeting should be held several weeks in advance to facilitate scheduling the attendance of invited team members.

Facilitator

A competent facilitator can make the difference between success and failure. The role of the facilitator is to lead the problem-solving process, control group dynamics, and guide process flow. Good facilitators keep the process on track, improvise process changes as required, sense the best creativity tools to apply, let everyone have equal time, and assist in harvesting team output. The facilitator leads the process rather than influencing content. The facilitator can be someone inside the company who has facilitator experience, a sound knowledge of creative thinking tools, and understands the problem-solving process. Alternatively, the facilitator can be an external consultant with a proven record hired to do the job.

Participants

Selection of participants is a critical factor in a successful team problem-solving session. The number of participants might vary from six to twenty or more, depending on the nature of the issue being addressed. In addition to the decision-maker and the facilitator, participants should include people knowledgeable about the issue, potential implementers of harvested ideas, and at least one "wild card." A "wild card" is a person known to be an energetic creative thinker, but not familiar with the issue being addressed.

Participants knowledgeable about the issue and with special expertise are essential. For example, a workshop addressing a plant groundwater contamination problem was successful because the design meeting included people with expertise in the oil industry. These experts were also knowledgeable about underground technology, which provided breakthrough ideas on how to cost-effectively remove groundwater contaminants.

Participants might have multiple roles. For example, an environmentally aware Catholic priest was invited to participate in a community meeting about how to reduce environmental contaminants. The priest was also meant to serve as a "wild card." He brought a fresh perspective to the issue, stimulated new insights in others, and contributed excellent ideas.

Depending on the issue, the team might include representatives from marketing, manufacturing, human resources, finance, technical, and business functions. Sometimes it is of value to invite special guests such as a customer, supplier, secretary or plant operator.

While thinking skills are important in successful problem solving, another essential ingredient is diversity. Hence, in selecting participants, attention should be paid to people with diverse thinking preferences, e.g., right versus left brain, and different creativity styles, e.g., adaptive versus innovative. This subject is dealt with in Chapter VIII., Diversity in Thinking.

Selecting Focus Areas

A vital step in the problem-solving process is to identify, within the broad problem statement, the "core" problem on which to focus creative thinking. This step is sometimes the most challenging. The purpose is to get as close as possible to the "core" problem, where idea generation is most likely to pay off. The team generally identifies many possible focus areas and then boils the list down to three or four. They decide on one focus area to attack, or they organize into separate teams, each choosing a different focus area. There are several effective ways to develop focus areas:

Wishful Thinking

This technique is popular with many facilitators. Participants are asked to think about a beneficial outcome related to the broad problem statement by completing the sentence:

Wouldn't it be nice if (WIBNI)?

For example, if the broad problem statement was:

How can we enhance our recruitment program?, A WIBNI might be:

Wouldn't it be nice if all potential recruits have personalized treatment during their visit?

The focus area would then be stated as:

How can we personalize the program for all recruits prior to and during their visit?

Barriers to Overcome

This technique addresses barriers to achieving a solution to the broad problem statement.

Participants are asked to complete this sentence:

What stands in the way of . . . ?

For example, on the problem of reducing waste in our forty plants, one question might be this:

What stands in the way of efficient tracking and measuring of waste? This question can be converted to a focus statement:

How can we effectively track and measure waste in our plants?

What's the "Real" Problem?

This technique simply asks the group to list what it considers to be the underlying problem.

For example if the problem statement is:

How can we spend less money on social welfare?

Possible underlying problems are :

- *Too much money is spent on administration.*

- *We need ways to get more money.*

- *We don't have ways to measure the results of our programs properly.*

- *People aren't qualified to get the jobs they need.*

- *What's the criteria for being on welfare?*

All of these statements can be converted into focus-areas.

Creative Problem-solving Grid

Reisman and Torrance often used the following quantitative approach to finding the "real problem." This approach may also be followed by finding the *best* solution.

Directions

1. Rank each possible future initiative vertically within each Evaluation Criteria (5 = most important/desirable/effective; 1 = least)

2. Add across Evaluation Criteria by row and enter sum in Totals column.

3. Consider the Positive Future Initiative with the highest score as your first activity to engage in.

4. If you are not comfortable with the Possible Future Initiative with the highest score, then consider the next highest. Remember, this grid is merely a heuristic (tool) for making a decision.

Creative Problem Solving Grid to Help Prioritize Your Activities.

Possible Future Initiatives	Evaluation Criteria							Totals
	Enhance Creative	Unique	Visionary	Attainable	Funding Source	Current Expertise	Other Grants	
1. NSF Proposal								
2. Create new course								
3. Write paper								
4. Implement new pedagogy								
5. Present at a professional conference								

"Peel the Onion" Pursuit

This approach is to dig deep into the problem until a level of abstraction is specific enough to be a good focus area.

Example of problem statement:

How can we increase yield in our fiber plant?

Peeling the onion sequence:

- Why is yield low? Because of broken filaments.

- Why are there broken filaments? Because of non-uniform polymer solution.

- Why is there non-uniform polymer solution? Because the ingredients feed system is not working properly.

Based on this "peel the onion" sequence, a potential focus area would be:

How can we get the ingredients feed system to work properly?

Trend Scenario

This technique is of value for issues such as:

How can we capture the owner-builder housing market?

The team would first list current trends in the market by asking:

What is happening now?

Then the team would list its views on the future by asking:

What are creative future possibilities?

Based on the possible future scenarios, the team can now develop a host of future needs or opportunities to form the basis for focus areas.

Point of View

In developing focus areas, the team can look at the problem from different points of view. For example, in tackling the problem:

How can we capture the owner-builder housing market?

The team can divide into groups to develop focus areas

from various points of view such as that of the homeowner, builder, and supplier. All focus areas can then be pooled, from which a balanced set can be selected for the idea generation step.

Harvesting Best Ideas

Harvesting best ideas is important in both types of problem solving described above. A creative problem-solving session will often generate 50–150 ideas posted on hang charts. This includes ideas generated by both pattern thinking and creativity techniques. The challenge is to harvest the ideas the team views as most worthy to implement.

The selection process varies. The team might formulate criteria such as business stake, feasibility, and uniqueness. Team members might individually examine the ideas and vote for the ones they consider the most valuable. The list often boils down to three to six ideas for further discussion. Finally, two to three ideas are usually selected for careful evaluation and upgrading before deciding on implementation.

The Six Thinking Hats framework, described in Chapter VI, is a powerful way to evaluate and upgrade ideas in a productive, effective way.

Implementing Best Ideas

Problem-solving sessions will be most productive if sufficient time is devoted to an implementation plan for best ideas. Otherwise, sessions are concluded with good ideas, but the ideas are lost when people return to urgent matters at their desks. This is why it is vital to have a decision maker participate in the session so he/she can assign resources, if appropriate. Each organization likely has its own process for implementing good ideas.

Implementing an idea

A format to implement ideas based on the Six Thinking Hats works well. The following sequence of hats is a way to plan actions influencing implementation of best ideas:

Yellow Hat
- *What factors favor the idea?*
- *Who would be supportive?*
- *Should we contact these people to gain early buy-in?*

Black Hat
- *What are the barriers?*
- *Who might oppose?*
- *Should we contact these people so we can understand their concerns?*

Green Hat
- *What are some ideas to overcome barriers?*
- *How might the original idea be upgraded?*

Red Hat
- *How do we feel about this idea?*
- *What is our gut feeling about whether we can get buy- in from others?*

- *Would we rate the current environment favorable or unfavorable?*
- *Should we act now or wait? Should we poll reaction?*

White Hat
- *What information do we have?*
- *What information do we need?*
- *How can we get the information that we need?*

Blue Hat
- *Next steps, responsibilities, milestones?*

Each hat stimulates thinking about what actions might be taken to implement the idea. This is a good basis for deciding on next steps. Many examples throughout the book describe how individuals and teams take the initiative to apply the tools described in this chapter to generate ideas that ignite bottom-line innovations.

In taking ideas to reality, several innovator characteristics described in Chapter V come into play. Sometimes the innovator takes steps to move an idea to reality as a one-person team. Other times, teams are involved where the innovator takes a leading position.

There are three core elements that work together in taking ideas to reality:

- The Innovation Team

- Leadership Sponsorship

- The Innovation Roadmap

The innovation team provides the horsepower for doing the work. The leadership sponsorship ensures support, strategic guidance, and an ongoing supply of resources. An innovation roadmap lays out the path for a team to follow. When properly structured, these three elements will reinforce each other and accelerate the rate of progress. The leadership effectively staffs the team. The team continually upgrades the roadmap. The road-mapping process prepares the leadership to supply resources to the team at critical moments.

A book by Charles Prather, Ph.D., *Managers Guide to Fostering Innovation and Creativity in Teams*, is an excellent book relative to the above subject and is highly recommended by the author (Ref. 26)

Critical Thinking and Logic as Essentials of Creative Thinking

Usually, creative thinking is associated with brainstorming (generating many ideas), novelty, and uniqueness of ideas. Critical thinking is analytical, judgmental and involves evaluating choices before making a decision. When you are thinking critically, you are using logic, reason and convergent-type thinking. As pointed out in another publication: [37]

...creativity involves creative thinking as a process of sequential interaction of two types of thinking – divergence and convergence as depicted in the figure below. Divergent thinking is the ability to elaborate and think of diverse and original ideas with fluency and speed (e.g., brainstorming). Convergent thinking involves narrowing ideas by evaluating the previously generated ideas that emerged in the divergent portion of the sequence (e.g., settling upon an idea from a selection of ideas)

Creative thinking process:

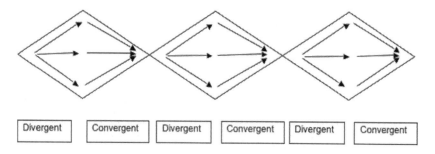

| Divergent | Convergent | Divergent | Convergent | Divergent | Convergent |

Idea Squelchers

Below is a list of idea squelchers that interfere with creative problem-solving. When reviewing the list, check off any of these comments you have a tendency to make.

We've never done it before.

We've already tried that before.

It can't be done.

It won't work.

Let's not reinvent the wheel here.

Too blue sky.

No way.

Are you nuts?

It's a waste of time.

I'm telling you, it won't work.

I just know it won't work.

What will the parents think?

Somebody would have suggested it before if it were any good.

Too modern.

Too old-fashioned.

Not that way.

Let's discuss it at some other time.

This is the last try.

You've got to be kidding.

You ask too many questions.

You don't understand our situation.

You don't understand our problem.

We're too small for that.

We're too big for that.

We're too new for that.

Let's not bother.

We have too many projects now.

It's been the same for 20 years, so it must be good.

This is how it's done.

Let's use proven methods.

What bubble head thought of that?

That's trouble.

Don't rock the boat.

We have to be practical.

It's not in the plan.

We did all right without it.

It's too early.

It's too late.

See? It didn't work.

It's not in the budget.

It has limited possibilities.

We're not ready for it yet.

All right in theory, but can you put it into practice.

Won't we be held accountable? Let's form a committee. Let's put it in writing. We need more lead time. Walk, don't run.

You'll never sell it to the union.

Don't forget the chain of command.

Stay on their good side.

Don't step on any toes.

Be practical.

Let's wait and see.

I don't see the connection.

It won't work in our department.

We can't do it under the regulations.

There are no regulations covering it.

That's not our responsibility.

That's not our department.

That's not our job.

That's not our role.

It's low in our priorities.

It will offend.

What's the use?

Why bother?

It doesn't matter.

Our people won't accept it.

You can't teach an old dog new trick.

Have you checked with...?

And you stand there saying...

No young person is going to tell me how to run this operation!

You can't argue with success.

It will mean more work.

If it ain't broke, don't fix it.

How to Squelch Squelching

1. Become "squelch" aware. Identify which idea squelchers you tend to use and work to eliminate them from your vocabulary.

2. Help your team/colleagues become "squelch" aware. Distribute this list to your team/colleagues so that they can become "squelch" aware. Brainstorm on what you can do together to stop using them.

3. Eliminate squelching from your meetings. Make it clear at the beginning of the meeting that squelching is not allowed. Put up a large sign saying "NO SQUELCHING" before starting the meeting. Make sure

everyone knows what you mean by squelching. Then, during the meeting, if someone does try to squelch (and it almost always happens early on), gently point a finger at the squelcher and say dramatically (but with a smile): "no squelching!"

4. Learn to fertilize ideas instead of squelching them. Catch yourself as the squelcher is coming out of your mouth and replace it with "That sounds interesting, tell me more." or "Help me understand..." Encourage ideas and help people think through their ideas with open-ended questions.

In other words: Squelch the squelchers before they squelch everyone's creativity.

Source: This list of squelchers was adapted from Chapter 2: Barriers, Blocks, and Squelchers: *Why We Are Not More Creative* in Gary Davis's book *Creativity is Forever*, 4th Edition.

Jazz Musicians as a Model for Creative Teams

Successful creative thinkers invent the concept and bring it to reality. Risk-Taking abounds

A novel tape, featuring Bobby Bradford & friends, was recorded by Stan Gryskiewicz, at the Center for Creative Leadership that provides a fascinating perspective about spontaneous innovation and creative teams (Ref. 27). Some points are applicable to dynamic industrial and healthcare teams, and others unlikely, except in unusual situations.

Key points:

- Innovation does not occur in a vacuum

  - Street musicians blended African and European musical forms - Result was "the blues."

- Goal and Role Clarity are Key

  - The leader assembles a group with musical competencies.

- The leader does not write down the notes or tell each member when to play each note.

- Goal clarity of the group is essential, but each player exercises individuality and improvisation.

- The leader is continuously balancing tension between team and individual behavior.

- Risk-Taking Abounds

  - Team members are encouraged to improvise creatively.

  - "Control" is partially lost and mistakes made.

  - The group expects mistakes and prepares itself to "dance on a slippery floor."

- Successful innovations lead to successful imitations.

  - Successful imitators creatively reconcile the new musical ideas with music "to which the public could dance."

  - Many variations on the new theme.

- An individual can make profound changes in the world.

  - Charlie Parker, Louis Armstrong, Duke Ellington

- Successful creative thinkers invent the concept and bring it to reality.

  - First reaction to something new is to squelch it.

  - Be-bop in original form sounded like playing with "a mouthful of hot rice." It opened the door to further advances.

VIII.

DIVERSITY IN THINKING PREFERENCES AND STYLES

Diversity in thinking strengthens potential for success in all endeavors

While creative thinking skills are important in successful problem-solving and innovation, another essential ingredient is diversity in thinking. This is particularly important as teams are formed to move ahead with an important innovation.

What would happen if everyone on a healthcare project team, in congress, or on a board of education, had the same background, experience, held the same values, and possessed the same thinking preferences and styles? Certainly there would be a relaxed atmosphere, communication would be easy, and one would expect that decision-making would be quick and painless. The trouble is, quickly made decisions would yield only hum-drum results.

Teams that include people with different points of view work in an atmosphere that comes alive. They work harder at true communication, and decisions that are made are infinitely better because a number of points of view were considered in reaching them. Diversity in thinking preferences and styles always leads to more creative solutions in any group.

This chapter describes three frameworks that measure diversity in thinking, with practical examples: The Ned Herrmann Brain Dominance Instrument (HBDI) that measures thinking preferences, the Michael Kirton Adaptor/Innovator Inventory (KAI) that measures creativity styles, and the Reisman Creativity Assessment Process which assesses an individual's self-perception on 11 major creativity factors . These are not the only methods for assessing and describing thinking styles, however, they can provide useful approaches for steering groups towards more respectful and collaborative dynamics.

The Herrmann Brain Dominance Instrument (HBDI)

Ned Herrmann, an artist, a physicist by training, and a former manager of Management Education at General Electric, is the father of the *Brain Dominance Instrument* (Ref. 11,12). The instrument integrates the scientific study of the brain with the study of human development. This section briefly overviews the *Herrmann Brain Dominance Instrument* (HBDI) and its practical applications.

Ned Herrmann, writes:

> *The brain is specialized - not just physically, but mentally as well. Its specialty modes can be organized into four separate and distinct quadrants - each with its own language, perceptions, values, gifts and ways of knowing and being. We are all unique composites of those differing modes according to our particular mix of mental preferences and avoidances.*

Reprinted with permission, Frank and Ernest Cartoons ccThaves

HBDI Assessment Theory

The basic concept of the Herrmann model is a metaphor for the brain composed of four interactive quadrants, each representing a category of preferences. Combined together, these four quadrants represent the "Whole Brain" Thinking Model.

Whole Brain Model

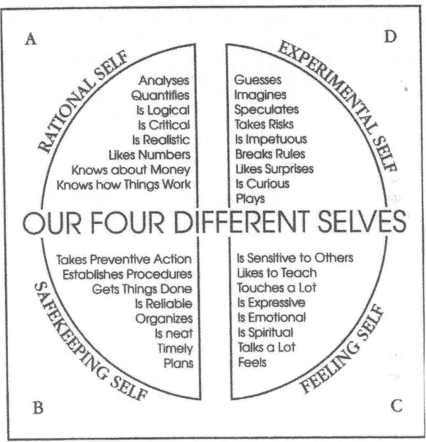

© 1997 The Ned Herrmann Group

Many people with strong preferences in the upper left (A) quadrant prefer performing analytical, logical, and mathematical activities and tasks. In contrast, people with strong preferences in the upper right (D)quadrant, prefer performing imaginative, intuitive, risky tasks and (or) activities. In other words, people with strong upper left (A) quadrant preferences may prefer to solve problems through reason and logic. People with strong upper right (D) quadrant preferences may prefer to think outside the norm, gets flashes of ideas, and to brainstorm and speculate to solve problems.

The two lower quadrants are the focal points of the more visceral forms of mental processing. Structured, sequential and organized mental activities are processed in the lower left quadrant of the brain(B). Emotional and interpersonal mental activities occur in the lower right quadrant (C). Taken together, the two cerebral hemispheres (A and D), and the two limbic hemispheres (B and C) form two different modes of thinking, which Ned Herrmann defines as our four different selves. For most of us, there is a brain dominance condition in which the quadrants work together, but with one or two taking the lead.

Measurement

The HBDI Assessment has 120 questions that measures the degree of thinking preferences in each of the four quadrants.

Herrmann Brain Dominance Profile

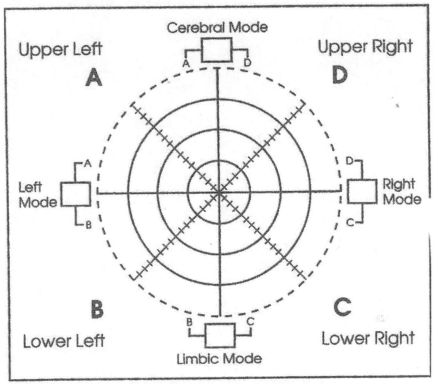

Over a million men's and women's brain dominance profiles have been assessed by the HBDI Assessment. The strong correlation between the HBDI profile and human thinking preferences soundly validates the theory. Representative brain dominance profiles:

Representative Dominance Profiles

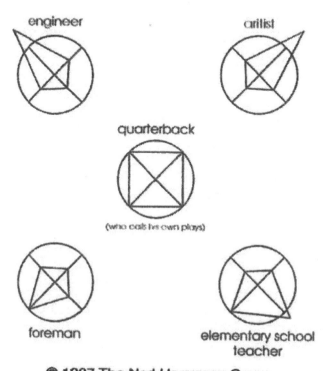

Whole Brain Thinking

Whole Brain thinking is particularly important in problem-solving and dealing with difficult challenges. The HBDI profiles of members of a hospital staff are good examples. In hospitals, the doctors, nurses, administrators, and psychiatrists each often have different primary preferences.

Herrmann Brain Dominance Profiles

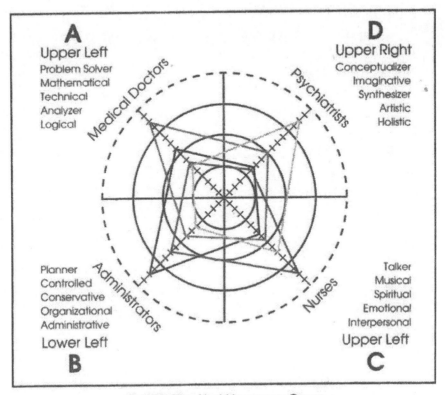

The average profile HBDI in the graphic above shows that doctors often scored strong upper left (A) quadrant preferences, nurses often scored strong preferences in the lower right (C) quadrant, administrators often scored strong preferences in the lower left (B) quadrant , and psychiatrists often scored strong preferences in the upper left (D) quadrant. Each group generally forms cliques in the hospital environment. However, in an emergency, since each of these preferences is essential to success , tribalism is suppressed and all work together effectively as a Whole Brain Thinking team.

Applications

There are many practical applications for the brain dominance concept, including the following:

- Interpersonal relationships

- Creative problem-solving

- Strategic planning team

Inter-Personal Relationships

Understanding the concept of whole-brain thinking and dominant quadrants is valuable in inter-personal relationships. It helps people to understand each other's thinking preferences and behaviors at work and at home.

Herrmann has described examples where marriages were saved by couples who took the HBDI Assessment and subsequently understood each other's thinking. For example, a husband who is anxious to decide rapidly on buying a particular easy chair, would normally be agitated by a wife who is meticulous about not making decisions, until she does a thorough investigation of all factors. The HBDI Profile helps him to understand that this is just her thinking preferences - that she is not agitating him on purpose.

Problem-Solving

The Herrmann Whole Brain Thinking Workshop, was one of the most beneficial I had participated in during the period of being educated in the field of creative thinking and innovation. About 20 people with diverse backgrounds, including a corporate financial manager, an educator, a computer specialist, a journalist, a human resources manager, a self-employed entrepreneur, and a sculptor attended the session. All participants had taken the HBDI Assessment in advance of the workshop but did not know results of their HBDI Assessment until toward the end of the workshop.

Most of the workshop was devoted to problem solving in a variety of situations and in mixed groups. The most fascinating session occurred when three separate groups were formed and presented with the same problem.

The only group that solved the problem had people with a mixture of thinking preferences in all four quadrants; hence, they tackled the problem with Whole Brain thinking.

Strategic Planning Team

The "Tyvek" Business Director had his staff take the HBDI Assessment to gain insights about the diversity of thinking in his team. To his surprise, his core group of strategic planners, consisting of a marketing manager, a domestic strategist, an overseas strategist and himself, had pronounced preferences, but supplementary differences in their brain dominances. One had strong preferences in the upper and lower left, A and B quadrants, another in the upper and lower right D and C quadrants, another in the lower B and C quadrants.

Together, these four team members had strong preferences in all four quadrants of the Whole Brain Model. From that time on, the director decided that he would not hold a strategic planning meeting unless all four of them were present.

The Kirton Adaption-Innovation Inventory (KAI)

Michael Kirton is a renowned British psychologist who pioneered The Kirton Adaption-Innovation Inventory (KAI). He related over dinner a delightful story of how, at the age of 7, he observed that two relatives consistently behaved differently when confronted with identical situations. This astute observation ultimately led to the widely applied KAI that measures people's creativity and problem-solving styles (Ref. 13). This section overviews the KAI and practical applications.

Basic Assumptions in the Adaption-Innovation Theory:

- All people are creative; everyone generates ideas (novelty); everyone problem-solves.

- As far as brain operation is concerned, creativity and problem-solving seem indistinguishable. The distinction may be little more than linguistic.

- Everyone is a change agent. This fits well into quality management where all are involved in quality operations.

- Adaption-Innovation theory distinguishes sharply between style (what way) and level (how good). They do not correlate. Everyone can be measured on Level: How creative am I ? or Style: How do I create?

- Level is related to skill, IQ, and competency, much of which can be improved by learning.

- Preferred style is unchanging throughout life, research shows. We can, however, learn to operate outside our preferred style by using coping behavior, when we acquire the insight that is needed.

- So, creativity is not always innovative or at high level.

The Adaption-Innovation theory postulates that people are creative and solve problems, to a greater or lesser degree, on a continuum of styles from *adaptive* to *innovative*.

The more *adaptive* prefer to make existing systems better; solve problems within existing paradigms; prefer a structured approach; are precise and dependable; and bring order and stability into novelty. The more *innovative* prefer to make existing systems different; solve problems with less resolve to existing paradigms; prefer an unstructured approach; may be unique and visionary; and risky.

A successful organization has a range of adaptors and innovators. Both can generate novelty. The former does it within the system, the latter with less regard to current practice, policy, systems, and paradigms. Everyone, regardless of where they fall on the Adaption-Innovation range, is liable to produce a new product.

The adaptor's product is more likely to be an improvement on an existing general model – doing the job better. The innovator's product is more likely to be radical – doing it differently. However, they all need one another. For instance, a highly innovative new product will undoubtedly need further development, especially from adaptors, who will strive to make it more practical and more cost effective. Most people are not at the extreme of either direction in the continuum but have a preference in one direction or the other.

Adaptors often view innovators as unsound, impractical, and a source of confusion, even if they are stimulating and challenging. Innovators view adaptors as conforming, timid, and stuck in a "rut," even if they are dependable, sound, and expert in detail.

A person's creative-thinking style is stable and related to personality. However, behavior is flexible. The ability to shift style under circumstances where shifts are desirable is termed coping. Some people are better able to cope than others, having acquired the insight that it is needed and learned how to do so. Understanding the Adaption-Innovation theory generally helps people to become more conscious of the need to cope, particularly to other styles in a team situation. They realize that the primary focus is to solve the problem with the help of others on the continuum rather than despite them.

Excluding Dr. Kirton's own work, scholars have written some 350 journal articles and over 100 theses using the KAI theory and inventory. This research comes from several countries.

Measurement

KAI, as a measure of the theory, is a meticulously researched psychometric inventory that yields a score that distinguishes the more adaptive from the more innovative on a continuum.

Styles of Creativity

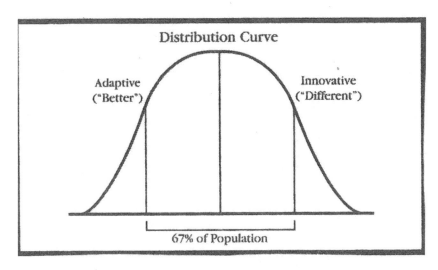

Published with the permission of Dr. M. J, Kirton

In filling out the KAI Inventory, consisting of 32 items there are no right or wrong answers. Preference for a more adaptive or a more innovative approach to problem-solving is not good or bad. Each has its own contribution in dealing with an issue. To obtain valid results, it is particularly important that answers represent how the person views himself or herself to be—not as he or she wants to be, or wants others to perceive him or her to be.

A purpose of the KAI is to help individuals understand their own and other people's preferences and behavior patterns. This aids relationships and performance.

The KAI effective range is just over 100 points. People who know each other well can likely detect a 10-point difference in their scores. A difference of 20 points might lead to conflict and discomfort. Larger differences might lead to serious communication problems. Understanding others' differences leads to admiration and respect. Those who have an intermediate KAI score within any mixed team have potential to act as active "bridgers" as long as they are willing and have learned the needful skills.

Relationship of KAI and Six Thinking Hats Framework

The Six Thinking Hats framework, discussed in Chapter 5, Innovative Thinking Techniques, generally works best with a mixed group of participants who range, in KAI terms, from highly adaptive to highly innovative.

Regardless of the hat the group is wearing, a mixed group of adaptors and innovators provides a more balanced input to the thinking process. For example, in Yellow Hat thinking on a proposal, adaptors generally contribute important thoughts on the more obvious benefits, while innovators consider the proposal from different angles, contributing thoughts on less obvious benefits.

In Green Hat thinking, innovators generate more unusual ideas and concepts, while adaptors contribute ideas that are seen as more immediately acceptable. In Blue Hat thinking, adaptors are more comfortable and likely to be the ones to summarize the output of the session in an orderly way.

During the six hat discussion, the adaptors consistently follow the rules of parallel thinking, while the innovators often stray and require reminders. Generally, adaptors and innovators contribute equally to the successful output of the session.

Applications

There are numerous situations where practical application of KAI is of value including the following:

- Problem-solving; and coping

- Structuring a team; and

- Resourcing a task force.

Problem-Solving; and Coping

on potential participants in advance of the event. This helps form teams with a good balance of thinking styles. The best balance may differ depending on the nature of the problem or opportunity being addressed.

However, even ideal teams need to learn efficient In organizing a problem-solving workshop, it's beneficial to run a KAI coping behavior to be sure to manage problems not requiring the preferred style (and favored capacities).

Structuring a Team

A team of nine individuals had been selected from various locations across a large multinational company to initiate a creative thinking and innovation program. The evening before the meeting, KAI theory was explained. Each participant was given a KAI inventory, which each filled out, and it was scored overnight.

The morning involved much interactive discussion. After lunch, each individual's KAI feedback booklet was given to each respondent as his or her private property. They were also given a chart of the spread of scores so they then saw the distribution curve showing that eight of them were in the continuum of being highly innovative. Only one in the group was in the adaptive category. In the morning session, this person had been ignored in most of the interactive discussion. They agreed to share each others' KAI scores and learned which one was the lone adaptive person.

The afternoon's session took quite a different turn from the morning session. The team showed a great deal of respect for the adaptor and listened carefully whenever he had something to say in the interactive discussion. This team would likely have benefited if more than one adaptive thinker had been on the team.

Resourcing a Task Force

A senior executive was in the process of resourcing a task force to implement an important facet of an innovation-oriented strategic plan. He had heard about the KAI in a creative thinking seminar and requested that a KAI be run on his total organization to provide insights on selection of task force members.

The KAI showed that his organization was biased in the direction of adaptor, which he felt was generally appropriate for his business and consistent with his thinking style. However, there were a few individuals whose styles were innovative, relative to the rest. Recognizing the value of diversity in thinking styles, this helped guide him in selection of task force members, some of whom had been identified as more innovative according to the KAI.

Other Applications

Those familiar with KAI theory who take into account thinking styles of the organization leadership are in a better position to sell their ideas and gain financial support and other resources helpful in pursuing their initiative or innovation, whether adaptive or innovative. This is also of value as the leader forms teams, adaptive, innovative or mixed as needed, and interacts with supporters, adversaries, and recipients of the initiative.

Leaders familiar with KAI are conscious of the diversity of thinking styles in their staff group and act as a bridge, particularly in dealing with controversial issues. Sales people familiar with KAI theory might often plan a sales pitch based on their perception of the customer's thinking style. A salesperson having an extreme innovator style would have trouble making the sale to a customer having an adaptor bias or vice versa, unless the salesperson was able to cope with the situation and organize the pitch accordingly.

Educators familiar with KAI are conscious of the importance of organizing their lessons in a way that appeals to both the more adaptive and the more innovative students. The same is true of seminar speakers familiar with KAI who organize their presentations in a way that appeals to a mixture of adaptor and innovator audiences.

Readers of this book who want to gain further information about the KAI should view Dr. Kirton's web site: www.kaicentre.com. This contains information about a four and a half day KAI certification course, run since 1998. A team in Penn State University, the leading teaching center in the U.S. of this work, has set this course into a 9-credit, higher degree Problem Solving module, using the A-I textbook (2003; 2011) as the prime reference throughout. The web site also provides information about Dr. Kirton's textbook and latest publications.

The Wider Perspectives of Dr. Kirton's Theory of Problem -Solving

The following four paragraphs by Dr. Kirton are pertinent to the topic of this chapter and also provide added perspectives to the contents of this book.

The theory within which KAI is a style measure is that of problem solving. The brain developed in order to acquire what is needed to survive. It has the awareness to find (or create) within the environment opportunities to get what is needed and to manage (or avoid) what is hostile. It sets up the problem solving process from understanding the problem to finding and applying an appropriate solution and exploiting the outcome to achieve further success. This process (and others, i.e., creativity; invention) requires motive (the drive) to set it going in the right direction, at an adequate level, for the appropriate duration to complete the task. These cognitive elements constitute the strategy. The principal means are the appropriate capacities, each also at the appropriate levels (how good) and the appropriate style (in what way) needed to get the required solution to the specific current problem. This assumes, of course, that no specific capacity (or specific set of capacities) nor one specific style, at any one time during this problem solving process can always be the means of solving every problem. This need to continually select the appropriate means to solve a diversity of problems is one of the key learning needs of the brain, if it is to survive. When the brain has not the motive (often supported by collaborating emotion) backed by the appropriate levels and style, it has to learn how to acquire them and how to use them effectively, within the brain limits inherited.

Science is the highest means of acquiring the development of the needs to solve the problems that need solution. We must always be learning, as this book makes clear. Amongst this learning, then is that whatever solves one problem (or part of any complex problem) may not solve every other problem or every part of a complex problem. Yet our tendency is to believe that our existing knowledge (with modification) and our preferred style (with some flexibility) is the "best" start for every problem. But complex problems so often need a diversity of problem solvers, commanding between them the range of capacities and styles needed to solve this current specific common problem. That requires each member of the team, and particularly its leaders, to learn to arrange collaboration to make best use of their diversity to solve this particular common problem (called Problem A). Unfortunately, managing people not like us is not easy and requires more personal cost. So, the very diversity available to solve the problem may be the very diversity that pulls the team apart. It now becomes clearer that in (say) an engineering or finance problem, neither engineering nor finance, or even both, is likely to be enough). Equally, in a complex problem or a set of problems, is either adaption or innovation likely to be enough.

Capacities we usually understand better than styles. Adaption-innovation is a range on the one hand preferring solving problems by first setting each one into a consensually conceived paradigm and using approved methods to resolve them. Adaptors, then, *bring about change as an outcome of solving the problem.* Their weakness is that if the current paradigm does not contain the answer they either need more innovative colleagues and (or) some learning and coping behavior to re-set the boundaries of the perceived problem. Innovators are at their best when the problem needs re-setting, so they *bring about change in order to solve problems.* Their weakness is that when the answer lies within the tight structure of the current, consensually agreed paradigm (like a new element in the Periodic Table – a Nobel Prize level problem) they find it more difficult to stay within it. Here is where they need those more adaptive, and to undertake more coping and learning.

In short, the Paradox of Structure is that all structure, including cognitive ones, can be enabling and simultaneously limiting. The limits help enabling when the structure is appropriate and limits tend to block change when different enabling is needed. So, the lesson offered by this theory is that we need to manage team diversity i.e., (those not like us), at the extra cost as that might be, in order to manage a diversity of problems to the reward of all within the team (Problem A). Unwillingness to mange such diversities (Problem B) is the cause of many a team split and subsequent failure. Once we can manage the diversity of others, then our specialized expertise (e.g., innovation) can be put to powerful, collaborating use, just as this book suggests. Further knowledge can be obtained from: "Introduction", on home page www.kaicentre.com. It is a resume of theory and the first section of chapter one of the textbook: Adaption-Innovation: in the context of diversity and change.

IX.

PROMOTING A CULTURE FOR CREATIVITY AND INNOVATION

The most compelling initiative for a leadership serious about building a more innovation-oriented organization is to promote a culture for creative thinking and innovation. To accomplish this it's necessary to educate employees in the skills of creative thinking and innovation, and create a supportive environment for them to practice and apply their knowledge on the job.

This chapter tells the story of how this was accomplished in the DuPont Industrial Products Division, a group of seven businesses.

The DuPont Industrial Products Division, in the late 1980s, was under severe competitive pressure. Basic patents covering technology for the growth businesses, i.e., Kevlar", "Tyvek", and "Sontara", were expiring. Mature businesses, i.e., "Nomex", "Teflon", industrial nylon and "Dacron", were leveling off. To maintain a strong competitive position there was a need to generate entirely new ideas and concepts. To accomplish this, it was necessary to foster a culture for creative thinking. Hence, steps were taken to enhance the environment for creative thinking and innovation and to educate employees in the skills of creative thinking.

Importance of a Supportive Environment

A supportive work environment for creative thinking and innovation is a key component in an organization striving to promote an innovation-oriented culture.

FRANK AND ERNEST® by Bob Thaves

Reprinted with permission, Frank and Ernest Cartoons ccThaves

A symposium in 1986, sponsored by the Center for Creative Leadership, headquartered in Greensboro, North Carolina, had a series of speakers discussing the importance of work environment. A summary of thinking that emerged at this symposium provided the following insight regarding impact of work environment on people's innovative behavior:

> *It's insufficient for an organization to have creative individuals. The environment must be structured for creative tension, positive turbulence around a vision, and the space and freedom for people to "dance with their ideas" without fear of mistakes.*

The impact of environment on people's behavior is vividly illustrated by the experiment described below. It was organized by the Washington Post as part of a social experiment about perception, taste and people's priorities. The Washington Post experiment is as follows:

> *In the Washington, DC Metro Station on a cold January day in 2007, a man with a violin played six Bach pieces for about 45 minutes. During that time approximately two thousand people went through the station, most of them on their way to work. After about three minutes, a middle aged man noticed there was a musician playing. He slowed his pace and stopped for a few seconds, and then hurried to meet his schedule. Four minutes later the violinist received his first dollar from a women who threw the money in the hat, and*

without stopping, continued to walk. Six minutes later a young man leaned against the wall to listen to him, then looked at his watch and started to walk again. After ten minutes a 3-year old boy stopped, but his mother tugged him along hurriedly. This action was repeated by several other children, but every parent without exception, forced their children to move on quickly.

For 45 minutes the musician played continuously. Only six people stopped and listened for a short while. About twenty gave money, but continued to walk at their normal pace. The man collected a total of $32. After one hour he finished playing and silence took over. No one noticed. No one applauded nor was there any recognition.

No one knew this, but the violinist was Joshua Bell, one of the greatest musicians in the world. He played one of the most intricate pieces ever written, with a violin worth $3.5 million dollars. Two days before, Joshua Bell sold out a theater in Boston, where the seats averaged $100.

In this experiment the people were in such a "hurried" environment that they disregarded an event that ordinarily would have been of high interest and value. It punctuates the importance of an organizational culture where a "hurried" environment does not impede people's opportunity to observe events in their surroundings that might have value in influencing future innovations. An innovation-oriented environment is one where people have time and space to think and work creatively.

The challenge of initiating a program to create an innovation-oriented culture, bolstered by a supportive environment for creative thinking and innovation is difficult. Human nature is to resist change, resist "another program" on top of current assignments. Announcement of a new program is often regarded as just another "whim" of current management. This would certainly be the case in an attempt to initiate a "creativity and innovation program."

It was decided to proceed with such a program, but in a way that would avoid the usual inertia. The approach taken was not to "announce" a creativity and innovation program, but to just "start doing" certain things. An action-oriented culture-change model, designed by a DuPont consultant was adapted to help achieve the goal of an innovative culture.

Culture Change Model

A culture can be defined by the four components, shown below, and changed by shifting these components:

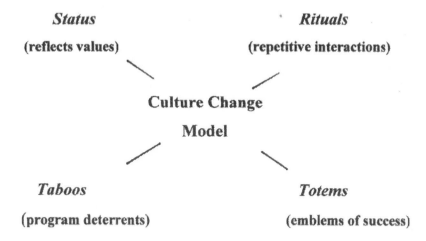

Status

(reflects values)

Rituals

(repetitive interactions)

Culture Change

Model

Taboos

(program deterrents)

Totems

(emblems of success)

1. **Status** is where we are grounded. Giving *status* to an effort reflects what management values. All other components must be coordinated and in concert with status. The *rituals*, *totems*, and *taboos* are functions of *status*, often overlapping.

Support of creative behavior by all levels of leadership is vital to success. *Status* expressed by the top leadership is important because it sets direction and priorities. *Status* given by middle and frontline leadership is even more important because they set local priorities, are involved in day-to-day operations, and participate in evaluating employee performance.

The Importance of Leadership

Reprinted with permission, Frank and Ernest Cartoons ccThaves

Top Management Support - Fletcher Challenge Limited was, until its restructuring in 2001, one of New Zealand's largest companies, with global operations in the building, paper, forest, and energy sectors. David Sixton served as CEO of the Building Products Division, the largest division of Fletcher Challenge Limited at the time, when it implemented an impressive focus on organizational innovation using many of the strategies described in this book. Top, middle, and functional leaders were all involved in conferring status to this focus.

As top executive at Fletcher Challenge Limited, Sixton set the tone, as illustrated in his comments in a widely circulated newsletter:

> *Today, new thinking is becoming essential in business. It's the edge on the competition in terms of product development, new ways of doing business, and developing better systems for serving customers.*

Sixton gave *status* to the pursuit of new thinking by establishing the Learning Group, headed by executive Claire Eeles. The Learning Group was active in many ways, including the following:

- *Scheduling a series of seminars to educate employees in the skills of creative thinking. At every seminar, Sixton introduced the speaker and remained in attendance to visibly show his support and expectations.*

- *Organizing and training a facilitator network of more than 100 volunteers from the business units to facilitate creative problem-solving sessions.*

- *Communicating to all employees examples of successes that contributed to bottom-line business payoffs (and there were many).*

- *Conducting a "Creative Practices Survey" to determine areas of strength and weakness in the environment for creativity and innovation.*

- *Joining the American Creativity Association to tie in with a worldwide network that shares learnings and trends in the fields of creative thinking and innovation.*

This broad-gauged effort gave prominent *status* to the management goal of establishing a creative thinking culture as the basis for igniting bottom-line innovations.

Middle Management Support - Unit heads in the DuPont Industrial Products Division gave *status* to the value of creative thinking and innovation by periodically replacing important technical program reviews with creative thinking workshops. The workshops were led by a guru in the field, such as Edward de Bono, who taught lateral thinking. The organization was receptive to this because it meant less work than preparing technical reviews. The substitution emphasized the workshops' significance.

In the morning, the invited speaker described tools of creative thinking and their value in solving difficult problems and sparking new innovations. In the afternoon, cross-functional teams composed of technical, manufacturing, marketing, and business people assembled in advance of the meeting and applied what they had learned in the morning to problems they were currently working on. Did each team solve its problem?

No. But making the effort did introduce them to the creativity field and its value in helping them think more creatively in problem solving and opportunity searching.

Employees became motivated to learn more. They began to read books on the subject and request permission to attend external seminars and workshops. Site libraries began stocking pertinent books and publications. The education process was underway for this "unannounced" program.

Functional Leadership Support - Awareness and value of creative thinking techniques in the Industrial Products Division spread from R&D units to manufacturing, marketing, and business functions. Divisional directors formulated a widely publicized divisional vision that gave immense *status* to the effort:

- *Creativity and innovation are valued at all levels in the organization, and management behavior consistently signals and reinforces this value.*

- *Employees are knowledgeable about the technology of creativity and innovation and are applying the skills they develop.*

- *Employees have the space and take the time to be more creative.*

Actions were taken to form multifunctional teams to implement the vision and periodically report progress to the leadership team.

Further *status* was gained by appointing a Divisional Creativity Manager, who became thoroughly versed in creative thinking techniques by attending many seminars and workshops. He communicated knowledge in the field of creative thinking and innovation and co-facilitated creative problem-solving sessions with the Divisional Facilitator.

2. *Rituals* are Many repetitive interactions initiated by management and site innovation champions to help foster a creative thinking culture. These included:

- Creativity Social Hours

- Green Hat Creativity Hours

- Principles of Effective Thinking Workshop

- Creativity & Innovation Newsletters

- Special Events.

Creativity Social Hours - An effective way to cascade creative thinking awareness in the organization was to hold *Creativity Social Hours* during monthly visits of management to R&D technical unit sites. These coffee-and-cake sessions were held at the end of the day following program reviews. In advance of the visit, each unit head was requested to invite two or three individuals in the unit to speak about a creative idea they had conceived in their program, and were now implementing.

This ritual stimulated the unit head to think about whom in his organization was doing creative work that merited recognition. During weekly staff meetings he began asking his group managers - *who in your group has been doing creative work lately?* This had the effect of cascading through the management line and increased awareness and interest in creative work being done in his group.

The highlight of these *social hours* was the enthusiasm expressed as each speaker described their creative idea and how they were implementing it. It didn't matter whether they used a specific creativity technique. The main point was that they took the time to think about creative alternatives to help solve problems or seek new opportunities. Over a period of years, everyone invited to speak agreed to do so. People seemed to love to talk about their work.

Asking people to be creative is like asking a child to be good. They often don't know what you mean. Hearing colleagues describe how creative thinking helped their work gave meaning to creativity. The metaphoric thinking example, described in Chapter V, *Creative Thinking,* that led to a dyeable "Nomex" fiber innovation, was first aired in one of these *Creativity Social Hours.*

Engineers in the plant process units originally felt that creative thinking was mainly of value to research people. This changed when they heard a fellow engineer describe how a creative idea helped him increase the productivity of a manufacturing process under development by 20% versus the goal of only 5%. They now understood what creative thinking meant and how it might benefit them. Hence, they became more involved in the unit's creativity effort.

Green Hat Creativity Hour - Several units had periodic creative problem-solving sessions to apply and practice creative thinking learnings to issues needing a new line of thinking. One such group was the industrial nylon R&D unit at the Chattanooga nylon plant. They had been active participants in the creativity and innovation effort, and initiated a monthly *Green Hat Creativity Hour.* Their approach was to tackle difficult technical and manufacturing problems presented by colleagues, applying the Six Thinking Hats framework, which Dr. Edward de Bono had taught in a plant workshop.

Their creative thinking session would start with Green Hat generation of ideas to solve a problem presented by a colleague, using lateral thinking, and then evaluate best ideas using the Six Thinking Hats. In this way, they not only applied the techniques in group problem-solving, but also gained experience for future use. One example was to apply the process to create new concepts for collecting and stabilizing a new fiber under development.

Principles of Effective Thinking (POET) Workshop - One of the most effective rituals in the program to create an innovation-oriented culture was a POET workshop, organized by champion Jean Prideaux, Technical Group Manager, Kevlar Technical, with the help of several consultants.

The workshop was a hands-on, interactive experience that offered the opportunity to learn and practice creative thinking skills using the creative problem-solving process. Participants worked on real problems and opportunities they brought to the workshop, which was attended not only by R&D people, but also by technicians and plant operators and managers.

In one session, a team of technical engineers described a dead-end they had run into in scaling up a new process that had been demonstrated in the laboratory. The stake in succeeding with this new process was $30 million. They were ready to give up, but as a last resort attended one of these meetings, seeking help to solve this problem. Many ideas were generated using a variety of creativity techniques. The result was an elegant idea worth testing. It worked, and the development proceeded.

Creativity & Innovation Newsletter - A *Creativity newsletter* was issued biweekly by the divisional Creativity Manager who helped expand knowledge in the field. The newsletter was based on various sources and emailed to all divisional personnel and numerous others who were part of a creativity network across the company. An example is the "Honey Pot" story told in Chapter II.

Special Events - The Richmond, Virginia plant site, which had Plant Technical units in "Kevlar", "Nomex", "Tyvek", "Teflon" and industrial nylon, had an annual December creativity seminar/buffet to which all site technical and support employees were invited. The most successful of these had as the speaker, Dr. Annette Goodheart, a psychotherapist, who spoke about the connection between laughter and creativity.

When Dr. Goodheart was introduced to an audience of about 200 she began to laugh out loud! At first, everyone was stunned, but then realized that this was her way to shift from an apparently serious mood to one of fun.

Dr. Good heart' s main message was - *Take your job seriously, but yourself lightly.* She told humorous stories about her huggable teddy bear. There was a lot of laughter during her presentation. Miniature teddy bears were given to all 200 attendees. The following day, teddy bears showed up on many desks in the workplace as a reminder of the message.

Dr. Goodheart was also invited to speak in Wilmington, Delaware to an audience of DuPont managers and executives. The atmosphere was different than the plant site. Here, she wasn't as courageous, and didn't laugh when introduced. However, she did start off by commenting that *she wasn't accustomed to speaking to an audience where their pants matched their jackets.* Her presentation was well received, but not in the same spirit as it was at the plant site. Very few, if any, teddy bears showing up on desks the next day.

3. Totems are emblems of success that can be honored by reward and recognition. This is a controversial subject. Some believe that this causes jealousy and reduces communication among employees who feel others may use and get credit for their knowledge.

Based on experience in the Industrial Products Division, the benefits of reward and recognition outweigh potential negatives. This point of view is supported by the philosophy Rosabeth Moss Kantor, author of *Change Masters*. She wrote:

> *Rewards are often payoff centered versus investment-centered... unwillingness to bet on potential means that much potential innovation is lost.*

It was best to not wait until an idea reached commercial reality, but to recognize and reward individuals and teams when they generated novel ideas that were being successfully implemented in their programs. For example, in the *Creativity Social Hours* described earlier, researchers invited to describe their creative work enjoyed the recognition. Following their presentations, they were given gift certificates for dinner for two at a local quality restaurant, which was much appreciated.

Awards can vary depending on the value of the contribution. Some professionals prefer financial compensation, while others prefer additional freedoms in their work or attending external conferences of their choice.

4. **Taboos** are behaviors contrary to the values we seek to affirm, i.e., things that need to be eliminated from the culture.

Reprinted with permission, Frank and Ernest Cartoons ccThaves

In a culture of innovation, it's *taboo* to act negatively when a colleague suggests an idea, even if the idea appears to be outlandish. It's more productive to view the idea as a provocation that might lead to other ideas of value.

Another *taboo* is punishing employees for taking a risk that doesn't pan out. It's more productive to learn from mistakes rather than to punish.

The "Golden Egg" Award - A story pertinent to *taboos* is about a "Golden Egg" award that was described in one of the division's Creativity Manager's newsletters. The award was created by a small group of company presidents who met once a month for a variety of reasons. They soon found out that a favorite part of their meeting was the sharing of mistakes and other misadventures. The enthusiasm members felt for sharings led to the idea of a "Golden Egg" award. As one member put it, "I want to hear it from the member who got egg on his face trying out his idea." A trophy was soon put together (with the help of a "L'eggs" pantyhose container and some gold spray paint).

Presentation of this award for the best mistake of the month became a standard part of their meeting, and the trophy itself added an important new dimension. The winning president was expected to take the trophy back to his office and leave it on his desk for the entire month. The presence of the "Golden Egg" raised questions from visitors and led to telling the visitor how the award was won. It also gave the president a chance to be a model for treating mistakes as opportunities to learn how to do it better rather than as situations requiring blame. It legitimized the importance of learning from our failures, rather than using them to punish, and promoted the increase in trust, openness and creativity.

The framework below provides a vehicle to think creatively about ways to improve the environment for creative thinking and innovation:

Focus Area	Current Practices	Future Possibilities	Possible Actions
Status			
Rituals			
Totems			
Taboos			

The leadership and groups at all levels in the organization might address these questions:

- *What actions are currently being taken to give status to the effort? What are future possibilities? What actions might be taken?*

- *What rituals or repetitive interactions are currently in place? What are future possibilities? What actions might be taken?*

- *How do we currently reward and recognize successes? What are future possibilities? What actions might be taken?*

- *What taboos are currently being practiced? What are future possibilities to discourage these? What actions might be taken?*

Bottom-Line Results

The proof of the pudding is in the eating.

The *Oxford Dictionary of Quotations* dates this proverb back to the early 14th century. It relates to not knowing the outcome of an event until it actually occurs.

Over a period of time, the program to create an innovation-oriented culture in the DuPont Industrial Products Division led to many visible bottom-line successes. Many examples are described throughout this book, particularly in Chapter V., Creative Thinking Techniques. Three additional examples that stand out as testimony to - *the proof is in the pudding* - are described below.

IMPACT OF CREATIVE ENVIRONMENT ON INVENTIVENESS

Printed with permission, Frank and Ernest Cartoons ccThaves

Emergence of Champions

This example relates to emergence of a passionate champion who applied his learnings in a problem solving session that resulted in an annual savings of $6 million.

Jean Prideaux, a mechanical engineering Ph.D. and Technical Group Manager, "Kevlar" had no previous knowledge of the creativity and innovation field. One of the creative thinking tools he had learned in an off-site workshop was "stretch thinking." He applied this technique in a group meeting designed to set annual objectives for improving manufactured polymer uniformity, crucial in spinning a high-quality Kevlar fiber. The previous annual goal of 5 percent improvement was difficult to achieve. Jean suggested that the goal be a 50 percent improvement!

The group was stunned - they felt that this would be an "impossible" task. He asked why. The response was: *To do that, we would have to do this....* This type of "stretch thinking" set in motion a program that, as Jean put it, *failed miserably... the group achieved only 40 percent improvement.* The following year they achieved another 25 percent on top of that. The savings from this accomplishment was $6 million annually. This example of the value of creative thinking motivated others across the site to learn and apply creative thinking techniques in their programs.

Environmental Respect Award

This example involves a "Kevlar" Technical/ Manufacturing team that won a corporate Environmental Respect award that the manufacturing manager credited to the innovative thinking program.

The DuPont company established in 1990 a "Chairman's Environmental Respect Award" that was sought after by hundreds of DuPont divisions. The award was won by a joint effort of a "Kevlar" Technical/ Manufacturing team by reducing process waste in the polymer area by more than 80%, saving the business $3 million annually. The manufacturing manager wrote:

> *Many of the efforts undertaken by Kevlar team members were considered or attempted in the past without success. One of the reasons they succeeded this time is that Kevlar has had a program to change the environment for creativity and innovation and give to the organization the skills necessary to do their job more creatively.*

Patent Trends

One of the benefits of an innovation-oriented culture is that it inspires inventiveness. During the period that the innovation-oriented culture was enhanced in the Industrial Products Division, the number of filed patents soared. In the three-year period following initiation of the effort, notices of invention by R&D people surged from 40 in 1987 to 148 in 1989. In the same period, patent filings climbed from 16 to 67. Patent allowances nearly tripled from 10 to 28 and were on the rise.

Measurement of Progress

What Gets Measured, Gets Done.

Measuring progress in any endeavor provides incentives to get it done better. If it's measured, people pay attention to it.

Organizations that undertake a program to enhance the culture for creativity and innovation would benefit by measuring progress in the program. Two surveys that help to measure progress are described below.

Culture Survey

An *Innovation-Oriented Culture Survey* provides information on employees' views of the environment for creative thinking and innovation. It's a way to track progress toward the vision of an innovation-oriented culture. It's a questionnaire that contains sixteen specific questions and two general ones that are posed to members of the organization. The questionnaire provides feedback relative to the four components of the *culture change* model - status, rituals, totems, taboos - described earlier in this chapter. The survey is posted in Appendix 1.

The survey not only measures - *the proof of the pudding is in the eating* - but also serves as a platform for communication between front-line workers and the management. The results give management information about what improvements might be needed to motivate people to think more creatively, suggest new ideas, and work hard at taking best ideas to reality. For example, a survey might indicate that some people are dissatisfied with credit they deserve for contributions made in team projects. Steps would be taken to remedy the situation.

Innovation Trends Survey

This survey tracks progress in the flow of creativity-driven bottom-line innovations. It involves a five-step process that a management might follow to periodically measure rate and amount of innovation in all sectors of the organization. When publicized, it enables creative thinkers to share knowledge gained about success factors, potential pitfalls, and best practices. It raises awareness that innovations are valued by the management and expected. Another benefit is that it recognizes people and teams for their valuable contributions. The survey process is described in Appendix 2.

Facilitating Creativity in Higher Education

A massive 2006 measurement research report entitled *Facilitating Creativity in Higher Education: The Views of National Teaching Fellows by the Creativity Center Ltd.- was conducted by* Marilyn Fryer and described as follows:

As part of a collaborative program of research into creativity in higher education, the Higher Education Academy and the National Endowment for Science Technology and the Arts (NESTA), commissioned the Torrance Creativity Centre to undertake a study of the views of National Teaching Fellows (NTFs) in England. The views of 94 NTFs on creativity and its role in teaching and learning were collected through an email survey of all NTFs and interviews with 21 Fellows.

Creativity was seen as integral to the self-identity of most NTFs: all but three regarded themselves as creative and it was reported that creative teaching facilitates creative learning. The four aspects of creativity most congruent with the NTFs' definitions of creativity are: 'imagination', 'seeing unusual connections', 'original ideas' and 'combining ideas'.

The report stated that "there has been rather less investigation into the *views* of educators on creativity in teaching and learning. Prior to the mid-1970s the majority of such studies were based on Torrance's Ideal Pupil Checklist (Torrance, 1965, 1975), a measure designed to discover teachers' *attitudes* to pupils' creative behavior (see for instance, Torrance, 1965; Schaefer, 1973) rather than to identify 'ideal pupils' *per se*, as implied by the checklist name. This popular measure has continued to be used throughout the world (for instance, Von Eschenbach et al, 1981[38]; Noland et al, 1984[39]; Ohuche, 1986[40]; Fryer, 1989[41]; Sharma Sen & Sharma, 2004[42])."

Major findings of the study:

1. Most NTFs (92.2%) believe that creativity can be developed.

2. When asked to describe creativity in terms of their own discipline, results demonstrated that most of the answers could apply just as well to any discipline.

3. Most NTFs (60.6%) did not believe that the most academically successful students are also the most creative. Only 13.5% believed that they are.

4. Questions need to be asked about the relevance of current criteria for academic success. Do these encourage conformity and 'playing safe', for example? Do the criteria really reflect the kind of

graduates needed in the 21st century? If not, how should they be changed.

5. Further investigation is urgently needed to ascertain whether there are significant numbers of highly creative students who are not achieving high levels of academic success; and what steps need to be taken as a result of the findings.

In regard to the previous finding number three, Torrance observed:

Both Getzels and Jackson and I found that between the populations on intelligence tests and creativity tests, there is only a 30% overlap. In studies of academic achievement, and in follow-up studies of creative behavior, we found very little difference between the high IQ/not-so-high creativity, and the high creativity/not-so-high IQ. In fact, in most of my own studies, the high creativity/not so high IQ group achieved better than any other group. Thus we should make one of our missions that of getting research findings into practice.

X.

ORGANIZATIONAL SYSTEMS & STRUCTURES

This chapter describes three organizational structures and systems that were strong supports in a total innovation effort:

- Grass Roots Creative Thinking Network

- Center for Creativity & Innovation

- Creative Educator Network of Delaware

Birth and Growth of a Grass Roots Creative Thinking Network

This is the story of how an ad hoc group of seven DuPont employees began a *journey of a thousand miles* to enhance the environment for creativity and innovation across the company. The outcome was a corporate creativity network that, over a period of fourteen years, grew to over 800 voluntary members.

DUPONT OZ CREATIVE THINKING NETWORK

The DuPont Company
Oz Group
Helping Others Turn Dreams into Reality

Genesis

A *Business Week* cover story in late 1985 featuring creativity, stimulated interest to learn more about the creativity field, and how it might be applied to enhance divisional businesses. A group of seven employees from different parts of the company who were interested in creativity and innovation, were invited for dinner to share views about the subject. The group included Corey Ericson, Jim Green, Jim Magurno, Charlie Prather, Dave Tanner, Tim Weatherhill, and Nat Wyeth. The dinner was highlighted by a lively discussion about leading authorities, workshops and literature on the subject of creativity and innovation.

Most participants felt strongly that the company environment for creative thinking was weak. The group decided to continue networking and to meet again to take on the challenge of finding a way to enhance the environment across the company for creativity and innovation. *The journey to accomplish this seemed like a thousand miles, but we recognized that it must begin with a first step.*

The above meeting was the first of what later became the DuPont OZ Creative Thinking Network that grew over a period of fourteen years to over 800 members, representing all segments of the company.

The OZ name was coined in a second meeting of the original group that considered itself a "creativity pickup team on a bumpy, winding road toward a brighter future, as in the Wizard of OZ." This metaphor stuck.

Network Growth

As word got around, attendance at OZ meetings grew rapidly. The OZ Network *modus operandi* was based on voluntary effort. The only requirement to join was attendance of an OZ meeting.

The underlying factor for growth was a strong grass roots thirst to improve job performance through increased knowledge of creativity and innovation. Some asked permission to come, others just came. Bottom line successes, attributed to application of creative thinking techniques led some managers to encourage attendance at OZ meetings.

OZ Meetings

OZ creative thinking meetings were held every six weeks. They were convened and organized by a volunteer team of people with a passion to enhance the environment for creative thinking and innovation. Communication was through company email. At the beginning, 15-20 members attended. They took turns during lunch around a conference table sharing learnings acquired from articles, books and personal experiences. If a participant had nothing to share, he or she could choose to tell a joke, sing a song, or dance a jig.

As membership grew, half day meetings were held in the DuPont Country Club ballroom, often attended by over 200 employees. Management visibly supported OZ and its purpose by taking turns sponsoring meetings. A broad range of people attended, including vice presidents, engineers, secretaries, managers, scientists, marketers, accountants, lawyers and technicians representing most businesses and functions.

Speakers

A highlight of OZ meetings was audience interaction with invited speakers who presented seminars or conducted workshops on topics of value to OZ members. Examples of subjects covered: "Creative Problem Solving"; "Managing for Innovation"; "Whole Brain Thinking"; "Lateral Thinking"; "Green Light Thinking"; "Innovation in the Military"; "Advanced Creativity Techniques"; "Creative Imagery"; "Creative Leadership"; "Laughter and Creativity"; "From Research to Market"; "The Power of Positive Verbal Approach."

The "Are We Creative Yet?" Cartoon Book

The OZ Network championed several projects, including publication of a cartoon book, "Are We Creative Yet?." This project is discussed in Chapter XI.

Update

The OZ Network continued operating until the year 2,000, at which time the company was reorganized.

Center for Creativity & Innovation

To enhance creative thinking and innovation across the DuPont company, corporate management chartered a Center for Creativity & Innovation. This act was motivated by several factors and events.

Genesis

In 1990, Chairman Ed Woolard appointed two senior vice presidents, Bob Luft and Earl Tatum, to co-chair a corporate committee of senior executives to set strategic direction to renew the environment for creativity and innovation.

Committee members had little knowledge about the creative thinking field, but educated themselves through multiple interactive sessions with invited speakers. The session with Ned Herrmann and his daughter, Ann, stirred much interest in *Whole Brain Thinking*. Each member filled out the *Herrmann Brain Dominance Instrument* (HBDI), described in Chapter VI, *Diversity in Thinking*, and were intrigued by subsequent discussion of results.

The Chairman's annual world-wide Leadership Meeting included a status report on the committee's activities. The committee arranged for Ned Herrmann to be a presenter. He delivered a magnificent lecture explaining *Whole Brain Thinking* and results of the HBDI that all 400 attendees had filled out in advance of the conference.

In break-out sessions later on in the meeting, a portion of attendees applied the *Whole Brain Thinking* concept in a problem- solving session described in Chapter V., *Creative Thinking*. The issue tackled was: *How to educate*

DuPonters about the value of creativity and innovation? This created a lasting impression on participants about the value of the Herrmann model.

Another item in the committee's presentation, was a twelve minute video showing bottom-line impact of the *Industrial Products Division* creativity and innovation program. This video also stirred much interest. A video crew had been hired over a two-three year period to interview creative thinking champions and teams about successes achieved in the program to create a more creative thinking culture. Numerous examples were recorded from which six were selected to incorporate into the video.

The video included several examples described in other sections of the book. Champion Jean Prideaux described how he applied "stretch thinking," learned in a creativity workshop, to stimulate his group to generate ideas leading to a $6 million annual savings in Kevlar manufacturing costs (Chapter II, F). Another example showed the engineer assigned to develop a prototype process having a $30 million stake, admitting failure until a creative problem-solving session provided an idea that overcame the problem and allowed the development to proceed (Chapter II, B). A third example showed Floyd Ragsdale, manufacturing manager, explaining how the " dream" technique, learned in a Ned Herrmann creative thinking workshop, helped him to solve a costly plant process continuity problem (Chapter V). Other parts showed comments by engineers about the value of added space and freedom in helping them be more creative in problem-solving.

Another event in the sequence leading to the *Center for Creativity & Innovation,* was an Edward de Bono half-day seminar in the DuPont Playhouse attended by an overflow audience of over 1500 employees. His scintillating lecture included lateral thinking and the Six Thinking Hats. It was videotaped by a three-camera crew and selectively circulated to employees worldwide.

Following these events, corporate management originally decided to charter a *DuPont Innovation Center* to help spread the knowledge gained in the divisional effort across the company. However, since creative thinking techniques were the main ingredient in fueling new innovations it was decided that creativity must be in the center title.

Center Structure

The basic concept of the corporate center was to have in place a small core group that could reach out across business units, inspiring local champions to become actively involved in learning and applying creative thinking tools in achieving successful new innovations.

The center staff included a Director (David Tanner), a Creativity Manager (Charles Prather), and an Innovation Manager (Richard Tait). It also included three knowledgeable secretaries (Helen Snyder, Theresa Kardos, and Charlene Traill) who helped administer the effort and now had the title Creativity Associates.

The Center reported to two strong innovation advocates, Alexander MacLachlan, Senior Vice President of *DuPont Research and Development*, and Max Pitcher, Executive Vice President of the Houston-based Conoco oil subsidiary. Max Pitcher was marketing-oriented which sent the message that this was not an R&D program. The Center staff interacted a lot with the Conoco organization that later split off into a separate company. Their culture at the time was that "creativity" was for "strange" people, so contacts with Conoco focused on "innovative thinking."

The location of the director's office provided prestige for the mission of the center. It was located in corporate headquarters next door to Doc Blanchard, DuPont President, and down the hall from the Chairman's office. When Edward de Bono visited, he commented how pleased he was - he thought, jokingly, that the director's office might be located in a small basement space. The center budget was "unlimited," with guidance to spend whatever was necessary to get the job done. Perhaps it wasn't realized how many costly speakers, consultants and workshops were planned.

Center Location

Necessity is the mother of invention.

It was decided to locate the center's functional activities in the DuPont Building that houses corporate offices in downtown Wilmington, Delaware. But at the time the center was named, space was unavailable. It was time *to practice what we preached* and, out of necessity, be creative about how to establish a foothold in the building.

A tour of the building identified a wide hallway on the sixth floor with two small vacant offices, plus space in the hallway to house a receptionist's booth where Theresa could set up shop with a computer station. The hallway was converted into a library with reading tables, book shelves, and an eye-catching fish tank above which hung the Center logo.

The fish tank and center logo were visible as people exited the elevator and entered the hallway, which was now a Creativity & Innovation Center. Charlie settled in one office. The other office became a video room. Richard was located on the ninth floor, which had a conference room suitable for Center meetings.

The fish tank became a big issue. It contained live fish, violating building regulations. A safety inspector spotted the tank and requested that it be removed. Many nearby employees had become attached to the fish and objected. Through inaction, the tank remained without further ado. This was an example of *asking forgiveness, rather than asking for permission*, one of the teachings in a Gifford Pinchot workshop about creative risk-taking.

Center Operation

Center operations involved development of a mission statement, strategies to carry out the mission, and elucidation of center offerings.

Mission Statement

> *To catalyze the unleashing of the underutilized creative potential of our people, and to champion prompt implementation of best ideas to drive business success.*

Strategies:

- *Education of employees in creative thinking and innovation techniques.*

- *Application of the techniques to practical problems.*

- *Helping line managers establish a supportive environment.*

Center Offerings:

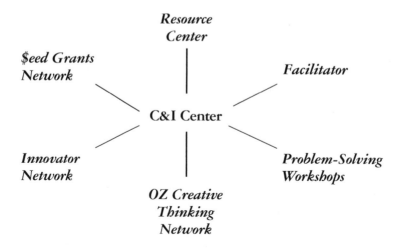

Resource Center

$eed Grants Network

Facilitator

C&I Center

Innovator Network

Problem-Solving Workshops

OZ Creative Thinking Network

Resource Center

A resource center managed by a creativity associate, was the focal point for email communication and scheduling of local and external seminars, workshops, network meetings and news items. It was the central point for business units to request problem-solving workshops to deal with problems or opportunities needing a new direction in thinking.

The resource center issued a semi-annual directory that included: a list of available books, journals and videos; calendar of internal and external workshops, seminars and conferences; list of facilitators available to lead skill-building and creative problem -solving workshops; and a list of seminar topics the center staff was available to present.

The resource center published a colorful brochure to highlight the offerings, suggesting that staffers call the center when they had one of the following impulses:

- A desire to improve your creative thinking skills;

- Important business or functional problems with no easy or obvious solutions;

- Customers you would like to help with problem-solving or finding new ways to use DuPont products; and

- A desire to enhance the level of creativity and innovation in your organization.

Skill Building - Scheduling skill-building seminars and workshops was a key function of the Resource Center. One stream of skill-building was in monthly meetings of the OZ Group, where participants shared experiences, participated in workshops, and heard many guest speakers.

Internal workshops included sessions with professor Edward Glassman of the Creativity College on creativity tools with emphasis on metaphoric thinking; Ted Caulson and Alison Strickland of Applied Creative Learning Systems on principles of effective thinking; and a series by Kim Barnes on developing the creative side, intelligent risk-taking and managing for innovation.

Seminars that were always well-attended were presented by Edward de Bono on lateral thinking and The Six Thinking Hats, by Ned Herrmann on whole brain thinking, and by Roger von Oech on creative block-busting. A frequently attended external workshop was Ned Herrmann's Applied Creative Thinking (ACT-1), discussed in Chapter VI. Internal skill-building workshops were frequently conducted by the Center staff and members of the Facilitator Network described below.

Facilitator Network

A vital function of the Center was to organize a network of facilitators committed to:

- Learning the skills of creative thinking;

- Championing these skills across the company;

- Facilitating problem-solving workshops in support of business units;

- Sharing experiences to help each other to grow;

- Participating in a volunteer pool that the Center could call upon as needed.

Within one year, the network had grown to over 120 facilitators from across the company. Some were full-time plant facilitators who were versed in organizational effectiveness processes and were eager to add to their offerings. Others were middle managers wanting to learn creative thinking tools and processes to apply in their units. Others were front-line doers aspiring to gain facilitator skills as a possible new career path. About 30-40 of the network became active, capable facilitators.

Training - Early in the effort, a core group of 30 facilitators attended a week-long workshop led by Edward de Bono. Here they learned lateral thinking tools and The Six Thinking Hats framework. Facilitators were encouraged to attend external workshops that certified them to use the materials and teach others. These included Dr. de Bono's lateral thinking and Six Hats workshops; Ned Herrmann's Brain Dominance Instrument; Michael Kirton's Adaptor/Innovator Inventory; and Scott Isaksen's Creative Problem-Solving Process.

A system of standards was established where a facilitator moved to different levels of competence. A facilitator-in-training moved to a higher level after experiencing a certain number of co-facilitations, becoming adept at leading the creative thinking process and applying creative thinking tools. The most capable facilitators were reserved to lead high-stake, business-oriented sessions.

Problem-Solving Workshops

Criteria for the center to resource a creative problem-solving workshop was the following:

- High business stake

- New direction in thinking required

- Participation of a person having decision-making authority.

The latter requirement was essential because if a good idea was identified to solve a problem or capitalize on a new opportunity, it would require assignment of resources. Otherwise, good ideas might not be pursued and the session would be a waste of time.

When a workshop request was received, an email message was sent to facilitator network members asking for volunteers. High-stake workshops justified a "Master Facilitator" and 2-3 co-facilitators. During 1991, the Center administered 78 creative thinking problem-solving sessions led by 19 Master Facilitators.

Success of a problem-solving workshop depends on the quality of the facilitator. A productive session led by a skilled facilitator adds credibility to the value of such a session and justifies the time and effort invested by participants. Success stories help increase business center interest in accessing Center offerings.

Additional discussion of creative problem-solving sessions and role of the facilitator is in Chapter VII.

Workshop Examples - Many examples of creative thinking workshops were discussed in other chapters. Three additional examples are described below.

Environmental Protection - This example illustrates how a creative thinking workshop aided engineers in a European manufacturing plant to accomplish environmental protection objectives along with financial and other benefits.

A manager in a DuPont European plant had received a copy of a video of the Edward de Bono half-day seminar given in Wilmington, described previously in this chapter. This led him to request a facilitator to lead a lateral thinking workshop to help them generate new ideas needed to improve environmental protection.

The session, led by Master Facilitator Steve Zeisler, provided creative ideas that helped the plant to eliminate all raw polymer waste, totaling 485,000 pounds in just six months. The process, according to the team, was to investigate each step that created raw material waste, then find a creative way to prevent this recurrence.

Overall, the team reduced manufacturing costs by $450,000 per year, reduced the plants energy consumption by 10%, and eliminated odor-related complaints from the surrounding community.

According to team members, their ability to find ways to do things differently was based upon training they had received in the lateral thinking workshop.

Reduced Groundwater Contamination - This example illustrates the importance of a design meeting in planning a workshop.

A plant was having a serious groundwater contamination problem. The estimated cleanup cost was $250 million over a five-year period. The plant manager requested a creative problem-solving workshop to tackle this issue:

> *How can we remove groundwater contamination at substantially less cost and time than current estimates?*

During the design meeting in advance of the workshop, an important idea came up regarding participants. The thought was that since oil people are knowledgeable about the earth's underground, wouldn't it be valuable to invite representatives from DuPont's Conoco oil subsidiary? Three people from Conoco gladly participated. Because of their presence, a breakthrough, low cost concept for removing contaminants from the earth was conceived based on technology for removing oil from the ground.

Polymer Supply Concept - This example illustrates how a creative problem-solving workshop helped identify technical objectives aimed at breakthrough new concepts for a polymer manufacturing process.

The polymer supply for a major corporate enterprise had been manufactured using basically the same process for 20 years. Ideas for major advances in process technology had been exhausted. The Enterprise

Chairman requested the Center to organize a creative thinking workshop with this problem statement:

How can we create a breakthrough in polymer "X" technology to recapture worldwide leadership?

In the design meeting, about ten employees from across the country were identified as participants with scientific and engineering expertise that might bear on this issue. Criteria for success was designed by workshop sponsors as follows:

The breakthrough idea idea should ---

- make a big difference in the business;

- lead us to the next step;

- be able to lead us to pilot plant stage by the year __;

- be of interest to people and fit their values;

- not prematurely limit current operations.

In the workshop, many focus areas were developed. The idea generation step and convergent thinking led to new concepts for four breakthrough - type processes. As a result. resources were assigned to pursue these new concepts. I learned some years later that a new process had indeed been developed embodying one of these concepts.

OZ Creative Thinking Network

This network, described earlier in this in Chapter had previously been administered by an ad-hoc committee. it was now recognized as a formal corporate network and administered and supported by the Center. This was one of the responsibilities of the center's Creativity Manager.

Innovator Network

One of the challenges of the Center was to establish a company-wide network of innovators who could share knowledge in creativity and innovation. To help accomplish this, the Center staff organized an event called the "Innovator Forum."

Innovator Forum - This event had these objectives:

- Raise awareness throughout the company that innovation was valued and expected

- Share learnings to help accelerate commercialization of new products, processes and best practices.

- Involve and honor people at all levels in the company for their innovative contributions.

A request for abstracts was issues with guidelines that the write-up track the innovation with a focus on basic business need; creative idea; the process of taking the idea to reality; and financial and other benefits. The "story" was to be told in a way that highlighted success factors such as creative thinking, sponsorship, supportive environment, risk-taking, and overcoming barriers.

The response to the request for papers was overwhelming. The Center received 265 abstracts from teams of innovators that included plant operators, mechanics, secretaries, engineers, marketers, and scientists. Essentially all business sectors, functions, and regions were represented, including Asia/Pacific, Europe, North and South America. Here is an example of an abstract received:

Is it Ivory or is it "Corian?" (Asia Pacific) - An international ban on ivory trading severely impacted an ancient Asian art form: ivory carving. A multinational and multicultural team did some creative thinking and came to the aid of these carvers. This impacted the community and provided the creation of a potentially new market for Corian. This market has potentially global impact for Corian as a substitute for ivory, and it was also consistent with the corporate emphasis on the environment. The impetus for the entire program came about through an individual's concern for the preservation of the African elephant. This program received no direct funding from the operating department, and all of the individuals gave personal time and effort to see that it came to fruition.

Forum Format and Award - At one point it was planned to have a large conference with presentations and a poster session. It was decided instead to recognize the innovators at local sites. This had the advantage of engaging a larger number of employees and was more cost-effective. Site management organized these events and played a key role in publicly recognizing innovators and their innovation, which was often the result of a team effort. An award with a "wave of Innovation" theme was designed and presented to 450 innovators participating in the forum.

The genesis of this award illustrates the value of diversity in thinking. Originally the plan was to use a miniature statue of "Rodin's The Thinker" as the award. This is what had been used in the Industrial Products Division's creativity effort. Helen Brown, a member of the Innovator Forum planning team, objected to the male symbol of "The Thinker." She was challenged to create an alternative of neutral gender. She came through with the concept of a "Wave of Innovation" award. Because of her creative contribution, she was the first to receive this award which was in the form of a miniature wave-like structure.

Poetic phrases accompanying video:

Upon a vast ocean of resources, creativity & innovation arise.

A resounding, perpetual motion, pressed by the constant wind of change.

New ideas rush to meet each other- taking shape and setting into motion a new wave of creativity and innovation.

The wave steadily sweeps across the ocean, quickly gathering momentum and strength; improving; growing; redefining its shape.

Soon the wave crests with the force of innovative change, exploding and releasing an energy that uncovers new resources - new areas for growth and improvement.

An then, the wave quickly flows back into the ocean; this time with a different kind of energy; an energy that will help create the next wave of innovation.

Forum Learnings - A summary report was issued containing abstracts summarizing innovations in:

- New Products and Applications;

- New Processes;

- Human Resources and Work Practices;

- Safety and Environmental Protection;

- Customer Interactions;

- Finance and Information Systems; and

- Continuous Improvement

Separate reports were issued in each of these categories containing the full papers and authors.

$EED Grants

$EED Grants was a corporate system that helped nurture ideas and innovation. The concept was that many employees were brimming with ideas, but they needed an opportunity, and a little bit of help, to implement their ideas. This program provided grants ranging from $5,000 to $50,000 to any employee regardless of level or function, who was committed to pursuing an idea and needed funds to do so. Developing the idea didn't relieve them of current job responsibilities. The ideas submitted were judged by a group of senior researchers who had moved up the research ladder and become Corporate Research Fellows. The program was administered in the Center by the Innovation Manager.

Center Update

The DuPont company has had many reorganizations in recent years. As a result, the center is no longer in place. However, the concept is timeless and other organizations have utilized many of the concepts described here.

Creative Educator Network of Delaware

This story relates how a state-wide educator network was formed and operated over a period of four years.

When the DuPont Center for Creativity & Innovation was announced, a reporter from the local Wilmington, Delaware newspaper wrote an article about the Center. It included this quote:

> *Creative thinking techniques are as important in the education system as in industry.*

As a result, the center was inundated by scores of letters, phone calls and visits by educators, community leaders and parents, requesting help to introduce creative thinking techniques into the Delaware school system. This led to a dinner hosted by the center where 29 educators attended.

An important insight that emerged during the dinner discussion was the need to teach educators the techniques of creative thinking in order for them to teach and apply them in the classroom. The outcome was a suggestion, seconded by most attendees, that a Creative Educator Network of Delaware be formed. The DuPont company's interest in contributing to community welfare led to implementation of this innovative idea.

The network was formed, meeting every six weeks at the DuPont country Club or at district schools. There were over 100 network members, although 20-30 generally attended. Participants included district superintendants, principals, teachers, parents, college and university educators and DuPont creativity facilitators.

Each meeting was co-convened by Steve Zeisler, a creativity champion, who also wrote and distributed meeting minutes. Each session featured a guest speaker covering a creativity topic. Topics included Ned Herrmann's Whole Brain Thinking, Edward de Bono's lateral thinking and Six Thinking Hats, Michael Kirton's KAI Inventory, Tony Buzon's mind mapping, metaphoric thinking, and the creative problem-solving process.

At several sessions, educators described techniques they had learned and applied in the classroom. On one occasion a teacher brought several students to demonstrate the creative thinking technique they had learned and were applying in class. The meetings always involved group interaction and sharing of experiences.

Prominent speakers who had been invited by the Center to address company employees, volunteered to speak interactively at the educator meeting. This group included Professor Teresa Amabile of Harvard, author of *Growing Up Creative*, Joyce Juntune, Executive Director, American Creativity Association, and Professor Leon Lessinger, University of North Florida College of Education and Human Services, also pioneering creative thinking in the classroom.

As the years progressed, the meetings took on the tone of more feedback from educators, who described how they were applying knowledge gained about creativity in the classroom. The network continued for four years.

XI.

IDEAS-TO-MARKET STORIES

This chapter describes how ideas are born and taken to market. It includes stories about:

- The "Kevlar" Innovation;

- The Crawfish Bait Innovation;

- The Are we Creative Yet? Cartoon Book Innovation; and

- Health Care Innovations.

The "Kevlar" Innovation Story

The "Kevlar" innovation story embodies essentially all of the creative thinking characteristics described in Chapter V., Role of Innovation Champions. (Ref. 28, 29)

Kevlar is a man-made "miracle" fiber five times stronger than steel at equal weight. Applications include bullet resistant vests and helmets; ropes and cables; sails; fire resistant fabrics; and reinforcement of tires, brake linings, and high performance composites in aircraft.

Creative thinking played a vital role in the discovery, development and commercialization of Kevlar. Importantly, many innovations were critical to the commercial development of the product, and many creative thinkers played essential roles. Together and individually, these creative thinkers exemplified the characteristics and roles of creative thinkers described in Chapter V.

The Need

In the early 1960s, the DuPont Pioneering Research Laboratory leadership, discontent with the status quo, envisioned a need for a super fiber with the heat resistance of asbestos and the stiffness of glass. The route to achieving these properties was perceived to be through stiff chain polymers.

The Discovery

A breakthrough occurred in 1965 when a creative research scientist Stephanie Kwolek found that the aromatic polyamide, paraaminobenzoic acid could be polymerized and solubilized under special conditions to yield a rigid-rod polymer. The polymer solution was opaque and watery in appearance. Conventional wisdom implied that the viscosity of the watery solution was much too low to be spinnable into fibers, and the opaque solution would plug spinneret holes. The experienced technician responsible for spinning experimental fibers steadfastly refused to waste time trying to spin this watery, opaque solution.

The environment in the Pioneering Research Laboratory was one that openly encouraged researchers to think positively, take risks, and buck conventional wisdom. Stephanie took a strong positive thinking position, insisting that something unexpected might happen. She vigorously insisted that an attempt be made to spin the solution into a fiber.

Surprisingly the solution spun well. We now know that the opacity was due to the formation of polymer liquid crystals that shear-oriented in the spinneret capillaries, yielding well-formed fibers with amazing properties.

Kevlar® Properties vs. Other Fibers

Reprinted from reference 28 and 29.

This discovery was the basis of what later became Kevlar and also catalyzed an entirely new field of scientific research. In 1996 President Clinton awarded Stephanie the National Medal of Technology.

Development

The Kevlar development had many hurdles to overcome. The raw materials used by Stephanie to demonstrate the concept were too costly to justify scale-up. Researchers developed suitable raw materials, but the spinning solvent for the new polymer had to be pure sulfuric acid. Sulfuric acid solutions presented a problem because they were too viscous to spin into fibers at economic speeds. To have a practical process it was necessary to lower the spinning solution viscosity. The normal approach would be to increase solution temperature, but if this was done, it was expected that sulfuric acid would seriously degrade the polymer.

A major breakthrough came when research scientist Herb Blades went against conventional wisdom. He took a risk and heated the solution to elevated temperatures. Surprisingly, the polymer did not degrade, but unexpectedly formed a previously unknown crystalline complex

161

with sulfuric acid. This invention, coupled with new spinning technology, improved spinning economics necessary for successful Kevlar commercialization.

The Manufacturing and Engineering Department people charged with designing, building and running a Kevlar plant took the position that it was impractical to build and operate a plant containing pure sulfuric acid. They insisted that it would be unsafe and corrode equipment.

Reprinted from reference 28 and 29

The researchers working on the Kevlar development were persistent about moving ahead.

When there is a will, there is a way.

They explained the unusual properties of Kevlar which could lead to many fruitful bottom-line business opportunities. This convinced the engineering and plant people to think more positively about how to deal with the difficulties posed by pure sulfuric acid. The project proceeded, leading to a successful commercial manufacturing plant.

Commercialization

The Kevlar plant was built in 1982 at a cost of $400 million based on a marketing forecast that Kevlar would replace steel in radial tires. This did not materialize. A "Fortune" magazine article called Kevlar - *A miracle without a market*.

That Kevlar did not replace steel in radial tires was a serious setback for the business. There was much concern about how to deal with this disappointment. Instead of taking a step backward and mothballing the plant, creative thinking management stepped forward with a strong positive view about the unique properties of Kevlar and its potential for entirely new product applications.

An intensive, unprecedented R&D program was initiated to search for new Kevlar end uses.

New Kevlar End Uses

In the search for new end uses, unexpected problems occurred. For example, one of the anticipated opportunities for Kevlar was to replace steel in ropes and cables. In air, the specific strength of Kevlar is seven times that of steel. In sea water, the specific strength is more than twenty times steel. Therefore, it was expected that one could use smaller, lighter, more easily handled lines.

Initial trials using standard rope constructions surprisingly led to Kevlar ropes much weaker than steel. Creative teams tried many alternative constructions and surface lubricants. The end result was Kevlar ropes having more than three times the life of steel in laboratory tests and more than five times in service. This experience led to the realization that the unusual properties of Kevlar would require identifying alternative designs for each end use application.

The challenge to develop new end uses led to many intriguing stories where positive thinking and persistence was an important ingredient for success.

The high modulus and thermal stability of Kevlar led to its consideration in reinforcement applications as an asbestos replacement. This was quickly ruled out by most "experts" because asbestos was cheap, and Kevlar was relatively very expensive.

Two staunch creative thinkers took a positive view that there must be a way for Kevlar to replace asbestos in spite of its higher cost. They tried many alternative approaches. The one that succeeded was development of a new form of Kevlar called "pulp". This is made by cutting Kevlar continuous filament fiber into short fibers having a very high surface area. Amazingly, only one percent of this new fiber form, uniformly dispersed in a base matrix, provided reinforcement equivalent to over fifty percent of asbestos. This discovery opened the door to major markets for Kevlar as an asbestos replacement in truck and automobile brake linings, gaskets, and hoses.

The outcome of the aggressive program to pursue new Kevlar end uses led to a variety of new products, including bullet resistant vests and armor that have saved the lives of thousands of law enforcement and military personnel. Today, Kevlar has hundreds of applications, including ropes and cables, sails, fire resistant fabrics, high performance composites in aircraft, and reinforcement of tires, brake linings and hoses.

The original failure of Kevlar to replace steel in radial tires was a *blessing in disguise* because this setback triggered an intensive R & D program, leading to many innovative new innovations.

Crawfish Bait Innovation Story

A "permitting" environment aids creative thinking in needs-driven innovation. This is illustrated in the Crawfish Bait Innovation story. This story also highlights several success-oriented creative thinking characteristics, and key steps in the innovation process, starting out with recognition of a need.

The focus of this innovation is crawfish, which for hundreds of years was a primary food source for people of French Canadian heritage living in the bayous of Louisiana. Many continued to live close to the water, where fishing and trapping were a way of life and income. In recent years, the popularity of crawfish and the Cajun way of cooking have spread nationwide. Cajun restaurants sprung up in many locations. Patrons enjoyed the flavor of the culture as much as the flavor of the food. All of that had led to a huge demand for crawfish.

The Need

Jay Daigle was a production worker in a DuPont plant but raised crawfish on the side. This part-time business was meant to be a relatively effortless source of additional income. But there was a problem—none of the available crawfish bait lasted long enough to make setting the traps worthwhile. Artificial baits could be used in the summertime, but they only lasted for a few hours. In the wintertime, the only bait was fish, but it was hard to handle and had many disadvantages. There was clearly a need for a long-lasting crawfish bait.

The Idea

Daigle had an idea that an inert polymer matrix might make the bait last longer. He took his idea to his friend, Mal Smith, who was a chemist. They formed a team and began bootlegging some experiments. They tested the samples at Daigle's crawfish farm. The results were encouraging, so they continued their pursuit of an improved bait. Because the polymer was not water soluble, they could provide farmers with a bait that would disappear only when the crawfish ate it. This increased bait life dramatically, from several hours up to as many as seven days. They talked with farmers, who were enthusiastic about the concept. Everyone wanted it - there was a market need for something they could provide.

The "Permitting" Environment

At first, the project was kept under wraps. Smith and Daigle borrowed time from other projects to develop their long-lasting crawfish bait. There was an odor in the back of the laboratory, but everybody looked the other way. Their supervisors must have known that they were doing something outside of their assigned jobs but never asked.

The inventors finally told people about their project. At first, people said it wouldn't work. The Plant Manager said they had invented the wrong thing. But when they explained their concept and its advantages, people offered help and volunteered to join the team.

The team's basic philosophy was that if they had a good product, they ought to get it into the marketplace quickly. They felt it would be best to refine the product in the marketplace rather than in the laboratory. They believed that the reason many products don't reach the marketplace sooner is that they are "tested to death."

"Warrioring" for Their Idea

Smith and Daigle went to the DuPont Agricultural Products Department, but they were turned down because crawfish bait didn't fit into its product line. They were persistent about moving ahead. It was up to the inventors to find their own way to market.

The team decided that the best approach was to make some bait and give it away to farmers to try in their traps and compare with other products. The trials were a success. The farmers wanted the bait, and wanted it badly. This demand created suction in the marketplace. The farmers called on the Agricultural Products marketing people requesting information about availability. Now the Ag Products people called for help in producing and selling the crawfish bait.

Bottom-Line Success

The giveaway was a huge success, and farmers came back for more. Crawfish bait was just the beginning. It was commercialized by DuPont as Aquabind® and sold into other markets such as binder and shrimp feeds. The technology and rights were purchased from DuPont by the two innovators, who formed their own company. Applications for the technology were expanded.

Learnings

The crawfish bait innovation is an example of a creative thinker having an awareness of a market need that could not be filled by competitive products. He generated a creative idea to meet that need and formed a team with another person who had the expertise necessary to explore and demonstrate the idea.

A "permitting" environment enabled the team to bootleg the project. It was kept quiet until the team had confidence that the idea would work and that there was a market for the product. They refined the product in the field rather than in the laboratory.

The inventors were persistent. They did not give up, even though the project had been turned down because it didn't fit into the established business. They "warriored" for their idea to keep it alive. In this case, they created suction for the new product by taking it to the marketplace and sampling potential customers. In the process, they leveraged the company image to add credibility to the development.

Finally, the concept started small but bloomed into a potentially large opportunity.

"Are We Creative Yet?" Innovation Story

Humor, or lack of it, can be an important source of new concepts that ignite new innovations. Humor was the driving force for publication of a creative cartoon book entitled *Are We Creative Yet?* This book pairs humorous cartoons with basic concepts in creative thinking and innovation. It was published in 1990 by the DuPont company (Ref. 4). A second edition was published in 2005 by *The American Creativity Association* (Ref. 5).

The Need
The story begins in 1987, when an ad hoc group of DuPont employees formed an *OZ Creative Thinking Network* with an objective to broadly disseminate concepts in creativity and innovation across the company. In the early stages of this network, monthly hour-long luncheon meetings were held to share thoughts and knowledge about creativity and innovation. The OZ name was coined during one of these luncheons when we considered ourselves a "creativity pick-up team on a bumpy road to a brighter future as in the *Wizard of OZ*." The OZ name stuck.

At one of these luncheons, Fred Dickson, a creative Patent Associate, came for the first time, and shared his thinking about the need to understand how creative people think, and how others can be taught this important skill. He felt that:

> *Most books on creativity and innovation were too vague, too lofty, and not much fun.*

The Idea

Fred noticed that many *FRANK AND ERNEST* cartoons by Bob Thaves had a creativity theme. He wondered whether this could be used to add humor to a serious message. His suggested that this might be accomplished by a cartoon book. This idea was reinforced by a phrase in the OZ Group's aim statement:

> *...to enable a culture for creative thinking and innovation in a way which is ... fun rather than drudgery.*

The group decided the idea was worth implementing.

Implementation

The first step, was for Fred Dickson, to travel to California to gain buy-in, permission and help of Bob Thaves. Having done this, the next step was for an OZ team to screen 6,000 *Frank and Ernest* Cartoons, from which 150 were selected as being pertinent.

A company-wide contest was held, with management support, soliciting short essays from employees expressing their views and experiences in the field of creativity and innovation that best fit the cartoons. The contest was publicized in the *DuPont Directions* magazine. Kits of the 150 cartoons were provided to entrants. Winners names would appear in the book. This cartoon/essay pair was published as an example:

Reprinted with permission, Frank and Ernest Cartoons ccThaves

The team approach to problem solving and communication will often lead to a simple solution to what at first may appear to be a complicated problem. Each member, including customer and supplier, is like the piece of a puzzle working with other pieces to better understand the situation. What looked like a "mess" can then become a success.

Over 400 essay/cartoon pairs were received from employees in over 25 states and 10 countries. The perceived 60 best entries, paired with 105 cartoons, were selected for publication. Pricing advice was obtained from the *Corporate Marketing Committee*. In-house printing and distribution were aided by a *Marketing Communications* OZ Group member. Legal agreements with the cartoon publisher were handled by an attorney who was an OZ Group member.

The cartoon book cover is shown below.

Cartoon Book Cover

Reprinted with permission, Frank and Ernest Cartoons cc Thaves

Examples of cartoon/essay pairs received from across the company:

The Importance of Teamwork

Reprinted with permission, Frank and Ernest Cartoons ccThaves

Successful problem-solvers know that what's important is to get the problem solved, not necessarily to get it solved solo. When you've come to a mental dead-end and need a better roadmap, leave your ego at a rest stop and ask others to help in navigating. Organize a team creativity session based on brain-storming, synectics, or other techniques. It's fun and mentally challenging. You'll be riding in the passing lane in no time.

The Importance of Gender

Reprinted with permission, Frank and Ernest Cartoons ccThaves

Some say that males are more "left-brained" and females more "right-brained." Problem-solving sessions are often more productive when there are male and female participants, possibly because of left-brain and right-brain preferences. But whatever the reason, try to include both sexes in your problem-solving sessions.

Commercialization

The cartoon book idea took three years to bring to market. The book was introduced in May of 1990 with the following forward by DuPont Chairman Ed Woolard:

There is plenty of room throughout DuPont for "heroes" in all types of jobs. We intend to provide hero status to those who show us how to get products to the maketplace more promptly and more creatively.

The OZ Group's Are We Creative Yet? cartoon book illustrates the creativity of our people and describes in a humorous vein some of the basic concepts in creativity and innovation.

By 1992, more than 20,000 copies were either sold internally or donated to educational and nonprofit groups, like the American Creativity Association. The decision to sell the books rather than to distribute them to all 140,000 DuPont employees was made on the premise that people value something more when they pay for it. The funds were used to cover expenses for speakers at OZ Group meetings.

Health Care Innovations

The Agency for Healthcare Research and Quality (AHRQ) sponsors a Health Care Innovation Exchange web site dedicated to providing information about health care innovations focused on patient care, and promoting their uptake and adoption. It includes creative programs in a wide variety of settings including hospitals, nursing homes, community clinics, schools, prisons and homes. The site focuses on new approaches to the delivery of health care services rather than on technological or therapeutic innovations. The web site *(www.innovations.ahrq.gov)* includes descriptions of over 500 health care innovations as of November 2010, has over 100,000 visits per month and over 40,000 subscribers.

This chapter contains three examples of health care innovations described on the web site.

Hospital at Home Care

The *Hospital at Home*sm program provides hospital-level care, including daily physician and nurse visits, diagnostic testing, and treatment in a patient's home as a full substitute for acute hospital care for selected conditions that are common among seniors.

The Need

Dr. Bruce Leff, Professor of Medicine at the Johns Hopkins University School of Medicine observed that hospitalization for older patients resulted in complications such as nosocomial infections and medical errors, as well as functional decline and delirium. He recognized the need to change the status quo and took steps to initiate a home- based hospital level care program with the potential to reduce these adverse outcomes.

The Needs-Driven Innovation

Dr. Leff implemented the concept of - *Hospital at Home Care* in 2001. The innovation was first piloted with 17 patients at the Johns Hopkins Bayview Medical Center where it demonstrated that the program was feasible, safe, and cost-effective.

The *Hospital at Home Care* innovation provides complete substitution of an acute hospital stay in the patient's home. Patient eligibility for in-home hospital care is assessed in the health care setting. Eligible patients are transported home by ambulance and receive initial and daily visits by a physician, continuous nursing support, home health equipment and services, diagnostic testing, and other services.

To evaluate the program in a broader range of settings, a study was conducted in three cities: two in Medicare managed care organizations in Worcester, MA, and Buffalo, NY, and one in a Veteran's Administration health center in Portland, OR.

A project team is working to disseminate the model to would-be adopters and developing protocols for *Hospital at Home* treatment for additional conditions, including urinary tract infection, urosepsis, volume depletion/dehydration, and deep vein thrombosis/pulmonary embolism.

Results

Studies have shown that the *Hospital at Home* innovation results in shorter lengths of stay, lower costs, readmission rates, and fewer complications than does traditional inpatient care. Surveys indicate higher levels of patient and family member satisfaction than with traditional care.

Use By Other Organizations

The New Orleans Veterans Administration started a hospital at home model in late 2007. Presbyterian Health Systems, a large managed care organization in New Mexico, plans a late 2008 startup for the program, while United Healthcare is planning to pilot the model in its Arizona market. Other Veterans Administration and Medicare managed care organizations are contemplating adoption.

After planning began in April 2007, Presbyterian Health Services, led by Lesley Cryer, RN, Executive Director of Presbyterian's Home HealthCare Services, succeeded in admitting its first patient to Hospital at Home in October 2008 and to date has treated 100 patients.

Other health systems around the country have shown interest and expect several additional major adoptions in 2009 through 2010. In addition, there has been strong international interest in the model.

Final negotiations with the Center for Medicare and Medicaid Services to obtain a waiver for Hospital at Home in fee-for-service Medicare are taking place. If that is successful, the model will be further developed at Johns Hopkins.

Aiding Teens With Chronic Asthma

This innovation improves care of young children and teens who are afflicted with asthma.

The Need

The San Mateo Medical Center cares for more than 1,000 children and teenagers with severe persistent asthma, most of whom live in poverty and are bilingual. Historically, these patients received uncoordinated care with little between-visit monitoring, causing high use of the ED and clinics when symptoms exacerbated.

Innovative leaders at San Mateo recognized a need to improve care for asthma patients and reduce unscheduled physician visits, ED use, and hospitalizations by identifying innovative ways to engage patients outside the clinic. San Mateo's clinicians, moreover, believed that having regular access to patient-reported data was the key to effective monitoring and their ability to provide focused, timely interventions to prevent acute exacerbations.

The Needs-Driven Innovation

The California HealthCare Foundation alerted San Mateo leaders to the BeWell Mobile Technology system and provided a grant allowing San Mateo to purchase the application and to fund cell phone service and the salary of an asthma care coordinator.

San Mateo Medical Center distributed mobile phones with customized disease management software to young asthma patients, allowing them to communicate with and receive real-time feedback from providers on at least a daily basis. The communication focuses on how to better manage asthma on an ongoing basis, with the goal of reducing exacerbations that might lead to costly acute episodes.

Results

An 8-month pilot test conducted at the San Mateo Medical Center found that this innovative initiative enhanced compliance with the daily diary and with medication regimens, which in turn led to better patient outcomes, less use of rescue medications, and fewer ED visits and missed school days.

Use By Other Organizations

Kaiser Permanente has implemented a BeWell Mobile Diabetes Assistant application with 84 adults diagnosed with type 1 or type 2 diabetes and poor glycemic control. Results show meaningful improvements in blood glucose levels. In addition, the University of California at San Francisco and Kaiser Permanente Division of Research have each used the BeWell Mobile platform and diary applications for patient-recorded outcomes in primary research.

Alzheimer's Patients Aided by Storytelling (Ref.)

This innovation uses group storytelling to enhance the lives of people with Alzheimer's disease and related dementia.

The Need

Alzheimer's disease and related dementia affects millions of individuals, leading to severe limitations for which there are few therapeutic options. Most long-term care providers (which are home to 70 percent of Alzheimer's/dementia patients) assume that these people cannot be helped. However, evidence suggests that parts of their memory can be stimulated and that encouraging communication can delay progression of the disease. An innovative approach was needed to capitalize on this evidence.

Needs-Driven Innovation

Structured weekly group meetings are led by trained facilitators to encourage persons with Alzheimer's disease and related dementia to use their creativity and imagination to create a story that can be shared with fellow residents and family members.

A volunteer or staff member leads weekly group sessions with 6 to 12 persons with Alzheimer's disease and related dementia. The meeting follows a very structured format, because such individuals still have their procedural memory intact. Participants, who are referred to as "storytellers," sit in a circle. Each meeting progresses as follows:

At the beginning of each group session, facilitators explain that the group is a safe place for storytellers to express themselves and that all responses will be woven into the story. Facilitators retell the story that was created the week before to reinforce the fact that participants still have the capacity to be creative and to combat those who say they do not. Retelling the story also reminds the storytellers of the structure of the group.

The facilitators share a staged photograph or illustration and ask the storytellers questions about what is happening in the picture. Facilitators are purposeful in the way they encourage participants to become storytellers, building on participant responses and using specially designed types of questions to further stimulate imagination.

Facilitators record all storytellers' answers, including seemingly nonsensical ones, on a large sheet of newsprint in an attempt to capture the emotion of what was said. If a storyteller contributes a response that does not seem to make sense, the facilitator repeats the response to the storyteller to make sure that they have captured it properly. Responses are recorded and crafted into a story either chronologically or grouped by clusters.

Periodically, the facilitator rereads the story that the group has already created; the goal of this exercise is to keep participants engaged and to help them expand the story. When the group completes the story, the facilitator reads it back to them, using the same emotion and enthusiasm that the storytellers themselves used. Once the story is completed, facilitators and storytellers celebrate what they have created by clapping, and the facilitators thank the storytellers for participating.

Results

Studies have shown that the Timeslips program has had a positive impact on persons with Alzheimer's disease and related dementia, leading to enhanced verbal skills and provider reports of positive behavioral changes, increased communication and sociability, and less confusion.

One study evaluated an 18-week program that was implemented in 4 adult daycare centers. Interviews with facility staff suggest that the program led to positive behavioral changes, increased communication and sociability, and less confusion. An analysis of the content of the stories found several common themes among participants, including humor and a clear desire for more freedom and human connection. In all four groups, storytellers engaged in the storytelling process as a method of self-expression.

Use By Other Organizations

Time-slips has 12 regional training bases across the country that are funded by a grant from The Commonwealth Fund. These training bases were developed to facilitate dissemination of the program throughout the nation.

Educator Innovations

Many innovations related to education have been described throughout the book such as the *Torrance Tests of Creative Thinking* (p. 19) and the *Reisman Creativity Assessment (p. 25).*

XII.

RELATED TOPICS

This chapter contains additional topics related to a Total Innovation effort:

- Human Resource Development

- Protecting Inventions

- The Power of Humor

Human Resource Development

Human resources play a vital role in operation of an organization that is striving to generate novel, useful ideas and take them to commercial reality as new innovations. Chapter IX, Promoting a Culture for Creativity and Innovation, describes a framework to enhance the environment for creativity and innovation. This section describes the importance of:

- Human resource interfaces; and

- Managing human resource growth.

Interfaces

A chain is as strong as its weakest link.

Human resources in an organization that has R&D, manufacturing, marketing and business functions must interface well with each other to accomplish business objectives. If one of the functions fails in its responsibility to interface effectively with one or more of the other functions, this would seriously weaken organizational productivity.

Role Grids

To help achieve excellence at functional interfaces, it's of value to develop role grids for key persons at the interface. Role grids is a process that helps individuals to mutually understand their roles while interfacing with others that they routinely interact with.

Two role grids provided by DuPont consultants Charles Krone and Sig Anderson:

- *Accountability Grids*

- *Mutual Responsibility Grids*

Accountability Grid

This grid specifies what a particular manager is accountable to the organization for. It includes a description of:

- What power or authority the organization invests in that manager's role;

- What control over resources the organization wants vested in that manager's role; and

- What actions the organization expects this manager to engage in with other people to accomplish the organization's business goals.

Mutual Responsibility Grid

It Takes Two to Tango

This proverb relates to a Latin-American dance where two people must dance in close unison for a successful performance. The proverb recognizes that there are certain activities which cannot be achieved singly, like arguing, having a marriage, or successfully carrying out innovative business objectives to achieve a goal.

This grid has entries that express the responsibility of each of two interfacing roles to each other. The key idea is that mutual responsibilities are the enablers of accountability by specifying those things that need to occur mutually between people to make the organization work as a business unit. The two people involved sit down together and develop mutual responsibilities. As an example, a mutual responsibility grid at the interface of a Technical Manager and Manufacturing Manager might have these components:

- Assist each other as equal partners in the business committee, but represent our own functions' needs and opportunities.

- Encourage participation in all phases of our functions' planning which might impact the others functions planning.

- Share jointly the responsibility to provide an appropriate arena and criteria for decisions on scale-up and commercialization of improved products and processes.

Similar grids would be developed between the management of all key interfaces, including: Manufacturing Mgr./ Marketing Mgr.; Marketing Mgr./Business Mgr.; R&D Mgr./Business Mgr.

Human Resource Growth

One of the most important imperatives in successful human resource management is to have in place capable developmental managers at all levels of the organization. These managers are key in shaping the development and performance of the doers in an organization.

Do unto others, as you would have others do unto you.

This proverb is the "golden rule." It's called the "ethics of reciprocity." It's roots are in a wide range of world cultures. It was present in the philosophies of ancient India, Greece, Judea, and China. The wording first appeared in English in 1567.

The "golden rule" is an important code to follow in human resource management, particularly at the manager-doer interface. Developmental managers play a vital role practicing the "golden rule."

There are many different management styles - looking up and looking down. A vital role of a manager is the one-on-one relationship with their people. There is a great difference between *developmental* managers and *self-oriented managers.* Developmental managers treat their subordinates' careers as they would expect to be treated by their own managers.

The *self-oriented* manager's priority is advancement of his or her own career. This kind of manager is reluctant to transfer best performers to other groups, even if it's in the best interest of that person's development and career. This type of manager is certainly <u>not</u> *doing unto others as he or she would have others do unto them.*

Supervisor Gene Magat, was an exemplary developmental manager. His management style at the manager-subordinate interface:

- Personal interest in subordinates well-being;

- Pinpoint areas for personal growth;

- Constructive suggestions;

- Recognize successes, critique failures;

- Supportive back-up when problems arise; and

- Strong advocate for subordinate's career opportunities.

Working for a developmental manager with these traits has a strong positive influence on an employee's performance and later on their own management style, if the employee's career path is up the management ladder.

An excellent description of the developmental manager's responsibilities is described in a book by Nils Dailey, *Profiles in Management - Roles of the Value-Adding Manager* (Ref. 34). This book describes nine roles of the *Value Adding Manager* including these four that are pertinent to enhancing subordinates' successes and advancement.

> *The Patron: As the patron, the manager provides the resources necessary to ensure the doers success, e.g., money, people , equipment,... access to influential decision-makers, and time..*
>
> *The Advocate: As the Advocate, the manager pleads the cause of the doers.... He can "run interference" and eliminate obstacles for the doers.*
>
> *The Devil's Advocate: As the Devil's Advocate, the manager challenges the doer's plans and actions... He encourages debate in order to explore a variety of perspectives. He challenges basic assumptions in order to test their validity. He provokes doers to anticipate problems and potential solutions.*
>
> *The Protector: As the Protector, the manager offsets the hostile and negative forces that can prematurely interfere with the doers activities. He courageously defends doers against attacks to stop them, especially when things are not going to plan.....*

An interesting exercise is to think about the best manager you've had and the worst. Then list and compare the manager's style of behavior at the manager-subordinate interface. This will serve as good input to one's own approach to management.

Protecting Inventions

An environment for creative thinking will inspire an increase in valuable inventions that have potential to ignite profitable new innovations. Inventions should be protected by an aggressive patent filing system.

This chapter describes a "patent excellence" program designed to energize the filing of patent applications in organizations seeking to protect their inventions. But first it will be of value to review the genesis of the United States patent system.

Genesis of the U.S. Patent System (Ref. 33)

In 1990, we celebrated the 200th anniversary of the U.S. patent and copyright systems. Our forefathers recognized that we were going to be a developing country, beyond just developing crops. They wanted America to be a place to grow and be great. They wanted to stimulate growth. President George Washington urged the first Congress of the United States to enact legislation to establish U.S. patent law.

The authors of the Constitution wrote Article 1, Section 8, which states:

> *Congress should have the power to promote the progress of science and the useful arts by securing to authors, for a limited time, the exclusive right to their respective inventions and discoveries.*

This group of words written in 1790 created the U.S. patent and copyright systems. Inventions in our country "flowed," creating new industries and jobs, fulfilling the Constitutional purpose.

Early Patents

One of the early patents was to Eli Whitney and his cotton gin. Donald Banner, former Commissioner of the U.S. Patent Office, historian, and past president of the Foundation for a Creative America, used to tell an interesting story about the cotton gin. The cotton gin was truly revolutionary, enabling picking 1,000 pounds of cotton per day, equivalent to output of hundreds of slaves per day. The cotton gin was so important that people wanted to steal it, so Eli Whitney kept it in his house.

One night, someone tried to steal it, so he jumped out of bed and created that famous American expression:

Keep your cotton-pickin' hands off my gin.

Other examples of important patents in the 1800s: Colt patented the revolver; Morse, telegraphy; Goodyear, vulcanization of rubber; Yale, the door lock; Howe, the sewing machine; Hunt, the safety pin; Borden, evaporated milk; Otis, the elevator; Westinghouse, the power brake for railroads; Bell, the telephone; Edison, the phonograph, light bulb, and movies; Eastman, the camera; others, the typewriter, barbed wire, and zipper. These are just a sampling.

In the late 1890s, a Japanese high official was sent to observe the U.S. He reported:

We have looked to see which nations are the greatest so we can be like them. We asked ourselves what makes the U.S. so great a nation. I have investigated this and found that it is patents; and we will have patents. (You bet!!)

Inventions change the world, bringing new opportunities, new products, and new strengths. It behooves the leadership of companies striving to build a more creative, innovative organization to pay attention to the filing of patents.

Patent Excellence Program

Protecting an organization's proprietary technology is aided by an aggressive patent filing process. This section describes a proven multifaceted patent excellence program covering these topics:

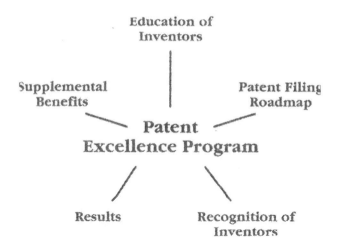

Education of Inventors

This facet of the program includes workshops conducted by people in the legal department. The aim is to familiarize potential inventors with their role in the patenting process. Methodology must include the proper way to keep notebook records, including recording of data, test methods, dates, inventor signature, and witness signature. If an employee believes he or she has made an invention, it is important to describe the invention and its relevance in solving a problem or creating a new opportunity, note differences from prior art, and record key technical elements of the invention.

Patent Filing Roadmap

Every organization should have in place a roadmap for filing of patents. The first step in a roadmap is for the inventor to write a notice of invention to the legal department. This is a description of the invention, including its perceived business value, how it differs from prior art, what problem it corrects or improves, how the problem was solved in the past, how the inventor solved the problem, and examples of how to practice the invention.

The next step is to form a team consisting of the inventor, a patent attorney, a member of supervision, and a business representative. The purpose is to assess merits of the invention and patentability. If the invention is judged to be of value to the business and patentable, supported by a literature search of prior art, then the attorney, with inventor assistance, drafts a patent application for filing in the U.S. Patent Office.

Recognition of Inventors

A key facet in a patent excellence program is recognizing and rewarding inventors. A monetary award is particularly motivating for inventors to do the paperwork required in filing a notice of invention and in assisting the attorney in writing and filing of a patent. The monetary award can be in two steps. Step 1 is an amount awarded for the filing of a patent (e.g., $300–500). Step 2 is a larger amount awarded if the patent is allowed (e.g., $1,000–3,000). If the patent leads to a profitable commercial product or process innovation, much larger compensation is often awarded by the corporation. However, this usually occurs many years after the patent is filed.

Results

One measure of success of a patent excellence program in an environment for creative thinking and innovation is the number of notices of invention, filed patents, and allowed patents. A patent excellence program of the type described above was implemented in the DuPont Industrial Products Division, a group of seven businesses, with rewarding results.

Reprinted with permission, Frank and Ernest Cartoons cc Thaves

Three years following initiation of this patent excellence program, concurrent with a creative thinking program, statistics related to patents soared. Notices of inventions submitted by R&D people surged from 40 in 1987 to 148 in 1989. In the same period, patent filings climbed from 16 to 67. Patent allowances nearly tripled from 10 to 28 and were on the rise. Results are illustrated in the diagram on the next page.

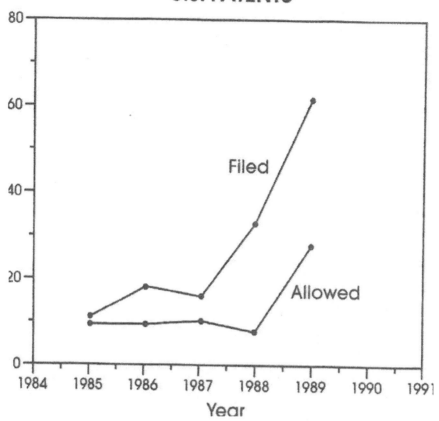

U.S. PATENTS

Filed

Allowed

Year

Supplemental Benefits of a Patent Excellence Program

The filing and issuance of patents is not just a numbers game. A patent excellence program also has less quantifiable benefits which are equally important.

Increasing awareness of the value of patents and encouraging research-ers to be proactive in the patenting process enhance thoroughness and efficiency of research. People become better at strengthening the validity of their data and gaining new knowledge. This in turn leads to an increase in ability to stake out and protect areas of importance to the business. The end result is an environment more conducive to results-oriented research.

A Tie Between Inventions and the Arts

There is a tie between inventions and the arts. Art and invention are often thought of as being worlds apart. Art is emotional and expressive and concerned with beauty. Invention is pragmatic and technical and concerned with knowledge. But there is a bridge. Both a work of art and a new invention are the result of a creative act. Both are the result of solving a problem in a manner that involves creative thinking.

Buckminster Fuller, the famous inventor, was asked about the relationship, if any, between these two disciplines. His response:

> *When I am working on a technical problem, I don't think about beauty— but when I am finished, if the solution is not beautiful, I know it is wrong.*

There is indeed a beauty, an elegance, a strong sense of art in every creative solution to a problem, no matter how technical the problem. If an original idea solves a problem, it might be the basis of an invention, and possibly a patent, that assures the future health of a business.

The Power of Humor

Humor is the most important phenomenon in the human mind. If computers could laugh there would be no need for humans to be creative.

Edward de Bono

This section describes: the relationship between creativity and humor; humor as the source of a valuable innovation; humor as a creative way to relieve tension; and the value of humor to coalesce people around a subject

Humor A Cousin of Creativity

The *punch line* is a crucial feature of every good joke and is related to creative out-of-the-box thinking.

Dr. Edward de Bono comments about humor in his classic book, *Serious Creativity* (Ref. 9):

Humor is by far the most significant behavior of the human brain. Humor indicates, better than any other mental behavior, the nature of the information system that gives rise to perception. This is a self-organizing information system. Humor not only indicates the nature of the system but also shows how perceptions set up in one way can suddenly be reconfigured in another way. This is the essence of creativity....Humor occurs when we are taken from the main track and deposited at the end of the side trap.

In humor, the mind trails linearly along the path of the joke, following our normal pattern of thought, which is then derailed by the out of the box punch line. Hence, the punch line is out-of-the-box thinking, like a valuable out-of-the-box idea. The humorous punch line is similar to a unique idea triggered by lateral thinking which was described in Chapter IV., Creative Thinking as a Skill.

A creative punch-line is illustrated below in a brief story a speaker might tell at the beginning of a lecture which is humorous and puts the audience in a relaxed mood:

Speaker: *Thanks for coming to hear my talk. I'm sometimes concerned whether anyone will show up. I heard of a story about a lecturer who expected a large audience, but only one person showed up. He leaned over and thanked that person for coming. The person said:*

   "Don't thank me, I'm the next speaker."

A Source of Innovation

Humor, or lack of it, can be an important source of new concepts that ignite innovations. Humor was the driving force for publication of the innovative cartoon book, "Are We Creative Yet?" This book pairs humorous cartoons with basic concepts in creative thinking and innovation. Chapter IX. tells the story of how the idea was born and the stepwise process of how it was brought to successful commercial reality. The cartoons attracted thousands of DuPont employees to read about concepts and experiences in the creativity and innovation field.

Tension Relief

Humor at the right moment in a meeting can sometimes completely turn-around a tense confrontation into a friendly positive direction.

The Fibers Department Marketing Director, Bill Harman, often met with important DuPont customers. On one occasion he visited Mr. Klopman, owner of Klopman Mills. The setting was a large boardroom conference table with Mr. Klopman at the head, attended by several executives from both companies.

The agenda item topping the list was the pricing of a DuPont fiber. This was important because it involved a large quantity of fiber for weaving into carpets. There was sharp disagreement between Mr. Klopman and Bill Harman on what would be a fair price. The discussion became so heated at one point that Mr. Klopman stood up and in a loud, threatening tone said -

If you don't meet my price offering, I will cancel all orders from Klopman Mills of DuPont fibers.

There was dead silence around the table. This was a tense moment!

One of the DuPont marketing managers stood up, and looking directly at Mr. Klopman said -

If you do that, we will cancel your subscription to the DuPont magazine!

Everyone in the room, including Mr. Klopman, broke out into roaring laughter. This bit of humor relieved the tension. It was a complete turn-around between supplier and customer into a friendly, compromising discussion leading to a pricing agreement.

Coalescing People Around a Subject

A *Joke of the Day* was issued daily via email to a network of thousands of DuPont employees by Jean Prideaux, Technical Group Manager, "Kevlar" R&D division, located at the Richmond, Virginia plant.

Jean was a champion of creativity and innovation and recognized the power of humor as a way to attract people's attention and coalesce them around a common goal. The daily joke not only started the day off with some lighthearted humor, but attracted people to read the emails which also contained news about creativity and innovation seminars, workshops and conferences. The *Joke of the Day* went on for several years. The source of the jokes were from numerous references.

Appendices

1. Culture Survey

This survey has fifteen specific and two general questions. It can be provided to individuals in an organization with the objective of gauging the environment for creative thinking and innovation. It helps to measure progress in a program designed to promote a creative thinking culture.

Survey

Please indicate the number corresponding to your perception of your working environment where, on a scale of 1 to 5, 1 is "too little" and 5 is "to a great extent."

<u>Number</u>

In my organization the leadership *encourages*:

1. Freedom for people to express new and controversial ideas that are welcomed and evaluated.   _

2. Training of employees in the tools of creative thinking and their practical application in yielding valuable innovations.   _

3. Challenging assignments which best fit people's thinking styles where some are best at generating ideas and others at taking ideas to reality.   _

4. Innovation in all segments of the organization including R&D, Marketing Manufacturing and Business functions.   _

In my organization there are these *repetitive interactions*:

5. Individuals and teams routinely apply creative thinking tools in problem-solving and opportunity-searching for new innovations.   —

6. Events are scheduled periodically with a creativity and innovation theme that continually energize the organization to participate in the program.

        —

7. People voluntarily attend creativity and innovation seminars and workshops scheduled periodically to help expand their knowledge in the field.   —

8. Schedules of creativity and innovation seminars and workshops are periodically communicated to network of interested employees.   —

In my organization there are these *emblems of success*:

9. People are recognized and rewarded for successfully applying new ideas to solve problems in their assigned program.   —

10. People are rewarded for suggesting creative ideas with business value outside their assigned program that are successfully implemented.   —

11. Stories of innovation successes are widely publicized through presentation at special events, email and occasionally by videos   —

12. Champions at all levels in the organization who utilize creativity and innovation tools are rewarded for setting the example for others.   —

In my organization there are these *deterrents* to creativity & innovation:

13. Risk taking is discouraged rather than encouraged, and punished if unsuccessful, rather than learning from failures and mistakes.   —

14. There is too little resource support to help solve problems creatively.—

15. People have little time to think creatively about new innovative business opportunities or finding new and better ways of doing things.   _

16. New ideas are ignored or discouraged.   _

General – List on back of page:

- The 2-3 most important factors in your working environment supporting creative thinking and innovation.

- The 2-3 most important factors in your working environment inhibiting creative thinking and innovation.

2. Innovation Trends Survey

The Innovation Trends Survey is a five-step process aimed at annually tracking the number and practical value of successful innovations generated from all units within the organization. The survey provides management with a measurement of progress, publicizes successes, shares knowledge about creative thinking and innovation, and gives recognition to individuals and teams. The process:

1.The company President or CEO requests Directors of the R&D, Marketing, Manufacturing and Business functions to identify and explain all innovations that have been accomplished in their organization in the past 1-2 years.

2. Each Director identifies successful innovations in their organization in the area of new products, new processes, human resources, work practices, cost reduction, finance, information systems, environmental protect, quality, etc.

3. Individuals and teams involved in each innovation are requested to submit an abstract describing the innovation with these guidelines:

- Describe the business need, the creative idea, the process of taking idea to reality, and financial or other benefits.

- Tell the innovation "story" in a way that highlights success factors such as creative thinking, sponsorship, supportive environment, risk taking, overcoming barriers and speed of delivery.

4. The innovation abstracts are communicated company-wide through email and/or written reports. This enables individuals and teams to share their knowledge and enthusiasm for the innovation process with others.

In some cases an organization might sponsor an event where teams present the innovation "story." This could be accompanied by award presentations if deemed appropriate by the management.

5. The Innovation Survey is conducted annually to measure progress and maintain momentum in the program to build a more innovation-oriented organization.

3. Proverbial Wisdoms

For the purposes of this book, aphorisms, adages, maxims, and epigrams are all sayings of a proverbial nature. Those included in this book are listed below along with their location in the book.

References

1. David Tanner, *Total Creativity in Business & Industry: Roadmap to Building a More Innovative Organization* (Des Moines, IA, Advanced Practical Thinking Training, Inc., 1997), (Tokyo, Japan, The Nikkan Kogyo Shimbun, Ltd., 1998).

2. David Tanner, *Igniting Innovation - Through the Power of Creative Thinking* (West Des Moines, IA, Myers House LLC, 2008).

3. David Tanner, *Health Care Innovation - Empowered by Innovative Thinking* (Rockville Institute, Rockville, MD, 2011).

4. The *Are We Creative Yet?* cartoon book (DuPont company publication, 1990)

5. The *Are We Creative Yet?* cartoon book second edition(American Creativity Association ACA Press, Austin, TX, 2005)

6. Alex F. Osborn, *Applied Imagination*, (Charles Scribner's Sons, 1953).

7. Alex F. Osborn, *Applied Imagination: Principles and Procedures of Creative Problem Solving*, (New York: Charles Scribner's Sons,1979).

8. Edward de Bono, *Mechanism of Mind*, (Des Moines, IA: de Bono Thinking Systems, Inc.).

9. Edward de Bono, *Serious Creativity,* (Des Moines, IA: de Bono Thinking Systems, Inc., 1999.

10. Edward de Bono, *Six Thinking Hats*, (Boston: Little Brown & Company, 1985, 1999).

11. Ned Herrmann, *The Creative Brain*, (Lake Lure, NC: Brain Books, 1988).

12. Ned Herrmann, *The Whole Brain Business Book* (McGraw-Hill, Harvard Business School, 1996).

13. Michael J. Kirton, *Adaption-Innovation: In the Context of Diversity and Change, 2005 (latest reprint,2011)* Routledge.

14. Edward Glassman, *Creativity Handbook: Shift Paradigms and Harvest Creative Thinking at Work*, (Chapel Hill, NC: The LCS Press, 1991).

15. Edward de Bono, *The Use of Lateral Thinking*, (Toronto: Penguin Books, 1990).

16. Edward de Bono, *Lateral Thinking for Management*, Penguin Books Ltd., 1971, 1987).

17. *Edward de Bono's Thinking Course*, (New York: Facts on File,1981, 1994).

18. de Bono Thinking Systems, www.debonothinkingsystems.com.

19. Tony Buzon, *Use Both Sides of Your Brain* (New York, Dutton, 1983).

20. Joyce Wycoff, *Mind Mapping: Your Personal Guide to Exploring Creativity and Problem Solving* (New York, Berkley Publishing Group, 1991).

21. R. F. Eberley, *SCAMPER,* (East Aurora, N.Y., Games for Imagination Development).

22. Edward de Bono, *CoRT Thinking*(Des Moines, IA, Advanced Practical Thinking Training, Inc., 1995).

23. W. J. J. Gordon, *Synectics* (New York, Harper Row, 1961).

24. George M. Prince, The Practice of Creativity (New York, MacMillan Publishing, Co., 1970).

25. Scott G. Isaksen, Brian Dorval, and Donald Treffinger, Creative Approaches to Problem Solving (Dubuque, IA, Kendall Hunt,1994).

26. Charles Prather, *Manager's Guide to Fostering Innovation and Creativity in Teams*, (The McGraw-Hill Companies, 2010).

27. Stan Gryskiewicz, *A Jazz Musicians Perspective About Creativity in Organizations* (Bobby Bradford & Friends Video Tape, Center for Creative Leadership, Greensboro, NC.).

28. David Tanner, Jim Fitzgerald, and Brian Phillips, *"Kevlar" - From Laboratory to Marketplace Through Innovation,* the DuPont company Advanced Materials International Conference, Wilmington, DE, November,1988.

29. David Tanner, Jim Fitzgerald, and Brian Phillips, *"The Kevlar" Story- An Advanced Materials Case History*, (Angev. Chem., Adv. Mater:, Nr. 5, 1989).

30. AHRQ Healthcare Innovation Exchange Web Site,

www.innovations.ahrq.gov/content.aspx? i =1787 *Hospital at Home,* Original publication August 18, 2008; Last updated October 7, 2009.

31. AHRQ Healthcare Innovation Exchange Web Site,

http://www.innovations.ahrq.gov/content.aspx?id=1690, *Aiding Teens with Chronic Asthma,* Original publication, April 18, 2008; Last updated, December 09, 2009.

32. AHRQ Healthcare Innovation Exchange Web Site,

Alzheimer Patients Aided by Storytelling, Original publication, October 27; Last updated July 21, 2010.

33. Donald Banner lecture, Washington, D.C., 1989.

34. Nils Daily, *Profiles in Management - Roles of the Value- Adding Manager* (Published by N. L. Dailey Associates, Guilford , CT, 1987).

35. Torrance, E. P. (1975) preliminary manual: Ideal child checklist. Athens, GA: *Georgia Studies of Creative Behavior*

36. Whitelaw, Louise A. (2006). An evaluative study of teacher creativity, use of the heuristic diagnostic teaching process and student mathematics performance

37. Reisman, F.K (December 2010). "Creative and Critical Thinking in Biomedical Research" *in From Getting Started in Research to Presenting Data in a Scientific Paper* (Eds. Y.K. Gupta, M.D., G. Jagadeesh, Ph.D.,, Sreekant Murthy, Ph.D.& Amitabh Prakash, M.D.). Wolters Kluwer Health (India), a subsidiary of Wolters Kluwer Health | Adis, Auckland, New Zealand.

38. Von Eschenbach, J. F. and Noland, R. G. (1981) Changes in student teachers' perceptions of the ideal pupil. *The Creative Child and Adult Quarterly.* 6, 3, pp.169-77.

39. Noland, R. G., English, D. W. and Von Eschenbach, J. F. (1984) Perceptions of gifted students and their education. *Roeper Review.* 7, 1, pp.27-30.

40.Ohuche, N. M. (1986) The ideal pupil as perceived by Nigerian (Igbo) teachers and Torrance's creative personality. *International Review of Education.* 32, 8, pp.191-6.

41. Fryer, M. (1989) Teachers' views on creativity. PhD Thesis, Leeds Metropolitan University.

42. Sharma Sen, R. & Sharma, N. (2004) Teachers' conception of creativity and its nurture in children: an Indian perspective. In M. Fryer (ed.) *Creativity and Cultural Diversity.* Leeds: CCET Press.

43. Reisman, F.K. and Hartz, T.A. (2010). Talent Management Handbook. 2nd Edition. EDITED BY LANCE A. BERGER & DOROTHY R. BERGER. NY: McGraw Hill.

44. Reisman, F.K. and Torrance, E.P. (2002). *Learning mathematics creatively: Place value.* Bensenville, IL: Scholastic Testing Service.

45. Torrance, E.P. and Reisman, F.K. (2000). *Learning mathematics creatively: Word problems.* Bensenville, IL: Scholastic Testing Service.

46. Torrance, E.P. and Reisman, F.K. (2000). *Learning mathematics creatively: Primes, fractions, decimals.* Bensenville, IL: Scholastic Testing Service.

47. Torrance, E. P. (1966). *The Torrance Tests of Creative Thinking-Norms-Technical Manual Research Edition-Verbal Tests, Forms A and B-Figural Tests, Forms A and B.* Princeton, NJ: Personnel Press.

48. Susan Cain, The Power of Introverts in a World that Can't Stop Talking,

49. E. Paul Torrance, *Psychological Inquiry,* Vol. 4, No. 3. (1993), pp. 232-234.

50. E. Paul Torrance, *Creativity Just Wanting to Know,* (Benedic Books Ltd, Republic of South Africa, 1994.).

51. Crabbe. A.B., E P Torrance. J P Torrance. D L Shewach. and G.J Shewach (1988) *Fourteen Years of Fuzzies.* Laurinburg. N.C.: Future Problem Solving Program.

52. Torrance, E.P. (1983) Manifesto for Children, Athens, GA: Georgia Studies of Creative Behavior and Full Circle Counseling, Inc.

53. Torrance, E.P., & Safter, H.T. (1990). *The incubation model of teaching.* Buffalo, NY: Bearly Limited.

54. Mayer, R. E. (1999). Fifty Years of Creativity Research. In R. J. Sternberg (1999). Handbook of Creativity. Cambridge University Press. Cambridge, UK.

55. Clymer, T., et.al. (1969). Reading 360 program. Lexington, MA: Ginn.

56. Clymer, T., et.al. (1976). Reading 720 program. Lexington, MA: Ginn

57. Torrance, E. P. (1979). An instructional model for enhancing incubation. *Journal of CreativeBehavior, 13,* 23-25.

58. Torrance, E.P. (2001). *Manifesto: A Guide to Developing a Creative Career.* Westport, CT: Ablex Publishing.

59. Wallas, G. (1926). *Art of thought.* New York, Harcourt, Brace and Company

60. Parnes, S.J. & Meadow, A. Osborn Parnes Model of Creative Problem Solving. *Journal of Educational Psychology*, 1959 - psycnet.apa.org

61. Csikszentmihalyi, M. (1996). *Creativity: Flow and the psychology of discovery and invention.* HarperCollins Publishers: New York, NY.

62. Amabile, T. M. The social psychology of creativity: A componential conceptualization. *Journal of Personality and Social Psychology*, Vol 45(2), Aug 1983, 357-376

63. Sternberg, R.J. (1986). *Beyond IQ: Triarchic Theory of Human Intelligence.* New York: Cambridge University Press.

64. Sternberg, R.J.(1998). *Handbook of Creativity.* Cambridge: Cambridges University Press.

65. Maslow, A. H. (1974). ***Toward a Psychology of Being.*** New York: Van Nostrand Reinhold Company.

66. Rogers, C.R. (1995). *On becoming a person: a therapist's view of psychotherapy*: New York: Houghton Mifflin.

67. Gardner, H. (1983). *Frames of mind: the theory of multiple intelligences.* New York: Basic Books.

68. Torrance, E.P. (1962). *Guiding Creative Talent.* Englewod Cliffs, NJ: Prentice Hall.

69. Torrance, E.P. (1985).*Why Fly.* NewYork: Ablex Publishing.

70. Torrance, E.P. (1979). *The **search** for **satori** & **creativity.*** Buffalo, NY: Creative Education Foundation Press.

71. Torrance, E.P. & Sisk, D. A. (1997). *Gifted and Talented Children in the Regular Classroom.* Buffalo, NY: Creative Education Foundation Press.

72. Torrance, E.P., Goff, K., Satterfield, N.B. (1998). *Multicultural Mentoring of the Gifted and Talented.* Waco, TX: Prufrock Press Inc.

73. Torrance, E. P. & Safter, T.(1999). *Making the Creative Leap Beyond.* Buffalo, NY:Creative Education Foundation Press.

74. Torrance, E.P. & Sisk, D. A. (2001). *Spiritual Intelligence: Developing Higher Consciousness.* Buffalo, NY:Creative Education Foundation Press.

75. Reisman, F.K. (1982). *A Guide to the Diagnostic Teaching of Arithmetic.* Third Edition. Columbus, OH: Charles E.Merrill.

76. Sawyer, K. (2013). *ZigZag: The Sustaining Path to Greater Creativity.* San Francisco, CA: Jossey-Bass.

77. Michalko, M. (2006). *Thinkertoys: a Handbook of Creative-thinking Techniques* (2ⁿᵈ Edition). Berkeley, CA: Ten Speed Press.

78. Michanek, J. & Breiler, A. (2014). *The Idea Agent: The Handbook on Creative Processes.* Second Edition. New York: Routledge.

79. Tanner, D. (2014). *Wisdoms to Live By.* Designed and printed in USA by CreateSpace.

80. Reisman, F. (1981). *Teaching Mathematics: Methods and Content for Grades K-8.* Boston{ Houghton Mifflin. (Reissued 1987 by Waveland Press, Inc., Prospect Heights, Illinois.

81. Reisman, F. (1977). *Diagnostic Teaching of Elementary School Mathematics: Methods and Content.* Chicago: Rand McNally College Publishing Co.

82. Reisman, F. & Kauffman, S. (1980). *Teaching Mathematics to Children with Special Needs.* Columbus, Ohio: Charles E. Merrill Publishing Co.

Index

About the Authors

David Tanner, Ph.D.

Dr. Tanner is former director of the DuPont Center for Creativity & Innovation, which developed and implemented innovation-fostering methodologies throughout the company. Prior to this, he held several management positions including Research Director, *Pioneering Research Laboratory*, and Technical Director, *Industrial Products Division*, a group of seven businesses including "Kevlar", "Nomex", "Tyvek", and "Teflon."

Dr. Tanner has a Ph.D. in chemistry, holds 33 early career U.S. patents, was president of the American Creativity Association and director of the de Bono International Creative Forum. He has authored four previous books: *Total Creativity in Business & Industry - Roadmap to Building a More Innovative Organization*; *Igniting Innovation Thru the Power of Creative Thinking*; *Health Care Innovation Empowered by Innovative Thinking*; and *Wisdoms to Live By - Expressed by Timeless Proverbs*. Dr. Tanner is currently an emeritus member of the expert panel of the government AHRQ Healthcare Innovation Exchange. (email: daveeet@aol.com).

Fredricka Reisman, Ph. D.

Fredricka K. Reisman, Ph.D. is professor and founding director of Drexel's School of Education. She currently is professor in the Goodwin College of Professional Studies and Director of the Drexel/Torrance Center for Creativity and Innovation. Additionally, Dr. Reisman served as Assistant Provost for Assessment and Evaluation and Interim Associate Dean for Research in the School of Technology and Professional Studies (SoTAPS) within Goodwin College. She is currently President of the American Creativity Association.

Prior to coming to Philadelphia, Dr. Reisman served as Professor and Chair of the Division of Elementary Education at the University of Georgia and as an elementary, middle school, high school mathematics teacher in New York State, and mathematics education instructor at Syracuse University.

Dr. Reisman has received external funding from several agencies including: US Department of Education; PA Department of Education; and National Science Foundation. She also collaborates on Drexel funded projects in the College of Engineering and serves as Co-Pi or external evaluator on several College of Engineering funded projects.

In 1984, Dr. Reisman headed the Drexel project management team for the Computer Applications in Teaching Program which was the first major effort to integrate computing into instruction in the Philadelphia high schools. She is currently in her third USDE funded Transition to Teaching Program bringing this funding to over $13,000,000 since 2002.

Dr. Reisman has authored several books on a wide range of subjects including diagnostic teaching, teaching mathematics to children with special needs, elementary education pedagogy, and mathematics pedagogy. She also has co-authored a trilogy of books with world-renowned creativity scholar and researcher, E. Paul Torrance, on teaching mathematics creatively. Dr. Reisman has completed a Grades 1 and 2 Diagnostic Mathematics Assessment that incorporates creativity theory published in 2009 by Scholastic Testing Service, publisher of the Torrance Tests of Creative Thinking. (email: reismafk@drexel.edu).

Made in the USA
Lexington, KY
01 July 2016